HOW TO WIN
AT
EVERYTHING

HOW TO WIN
at
EVERYTHING

EVEN THINGS YOU CAN'T OR SHOULDN'T TRY TO WIN AT

DANIEL KIBBLESMITH *and* **SAM WEINER**

★ ★ ★

CHRONICLE BOOKS
SAN FRANCISCO

Library of Congress Cataloging-in-Publication Data:
Kibblesmith, Daniel, 1983-
How to win at everything : even things you can't or shouldn't try to win at
/ Daniel Kibblesmith and Sam Weiner.
          page cm
ISBN 978-1-4521-1331-9
1. Success—Humor. I. Weiner, Sam, 1984– II. Title.

PN6231.S83K53 2013

818'.5402—dc23

                              2013008425

Manufactured in Canada

Book design by Tracy Sunrize Johnson
Cover design by Neil Egan and Tracy Sunrize Johnson
Illustrations by Jim Tierney

10 9 8 7 6 5 4 3

Chronicle Books LLC
680 Second Street
San Francisco, California 94107

www.chroniclebooks.com

The authors wish to dedicate this
book to the most inspirational
winners they know—themselves.

Introduction

Congratulations, Future Winner!

You hold in your hands a life-altering self-improvement manual guaranteed to turn you into the best person you've ever met. That is, until you meet us—authors Daniel Kibblesmith and Sam Weiner—geniuses of victory, gold-medal winners in the sport of life, and the writers of the most important book ever written.

Right now, you're a loser. Go ahead and look up "loser" in the dictionary—you won't find a picture of yourself, because they'd never print your picture in a book as important as the dictionary. But we can help.

Although you'll find it hard to believe, we were once losers ourselves. But by breaking free of the shackles of failure and slapping on the handcuffs of ambition, we've since amassed fortunes, traveled to ports exotic and cosmopolitan, and are the subjects of over 250 tattoos.

By tirelessly training in every human endeavor, we discovered the methods, techniques, and secrets to not only succeed at everything, but to *win* at everything—even at things you didn't realize you could win. For the first time, we're imparting our cumulative wisdom to you, the reader, to procure the success you may not deserve, but can now attain nonetheless.

Every line of this volume is worth the knowledge contained in ten encyclopedias, five almanacs, and seventeen Declarations of Independence. This practical, easy-to-digest reference book will transform you from child to adult, from scholar to genius, from rags to riches—and back. And then back one more time.

How to Win at Everything is an unrivaled reference manual spanning the breadth of all possible topics:

- **Winning a fistfight?** Check.

- **Juggling work and family?** Covered.

- **Representing yourself in court?** Yes.

- **Learning the date of your own death?** It's in here.

- **Finding true love?** We show you how.

Is this the longest book ever written? Probably. The authors do not claim to have read every other book. But we do claim that this is the last book you'll ever need, and it is therefore safe to become illiterate upon its completion.

The first step towards success? Turning the page.

The second step? If you haven't turned the page yet, you're clearly not ready.

—*The Authors*

Air Travel

Winners rise above the people around them—literally—due to a lifestyle that calls for constantly riding in airplanes. Overcome airport obstacles and inspire jealousy in the jet set with these secrets to flying high:

SAIL THROUGH SECURITY Hand the agent your ID, boarding pass, and a sincere thank-you note. Then breeze through the metal detectors by having on your person only paper money, wooden keys, and wicker underwear.

SCORE AN UPGRADE First class is for suckers who don't know about the secret *firster* class, replete with adorable puppies you can pet during takeoff and free blankets as soft as puppy fur during landing. Join this elite fraternity by slipping the gate attendant a blank check folded into a paper airplane.

SETTLE IN Don't bother reviewing the safety pamphlet (it's entirely theoretical, since no modern plane has ever crashed). Instead, go straight to the *SkyMall* catalog, call the number on the front, and order one of everything, plus a home subscription.

NEVER MISS A FLIGHT

Be sure to always arrive at the airport at least three hours early, so you have time to get your ticket, pass through security, and then purchase and read another copy of this book for two hours and forty-five minutes.

QUIET ANY AND ALL SCREAMING BABIES ON THE PLANE Impress fellow passengers and the crew by borrowing the onboard intercom to sing a soothing love song, but replace the word *baby* (sexual) with *baby* (literal).

DINE IN STYLE Don't be satisfied with a paltry bag of stale pretzels—ask politely to receive a *second* bag of stale pretzels.

LAND SMOOTHLY Get an exclusive tour of the cockpit by claiming to be nine years old—then subtly nudge the controls so that the plane lands right in front of your house.

GLAMOUR AT 30,000 FEET

COST-CUTTING MEASURES HAVE ROBBED AIR TRAVEL OF ITS FORMER GLAMOUR, BUT YOU CAN PUT THE CLASS BACK IN FIRST CLASS BY FLYING IN STYLE:

DRESS YOUR BEST Wear your finest tuxedo over your second-finest tuxedo or, for ladies, sexy workout clothes over an evening gown.

ENJOY A GOURMET MEAL If there's a McDonald's in the airport, you can take it on the plane with you!

FLY LIKE A MOVIE STAR Attract attention by shouting, "My last movie was a *bomb*, but they're still showing it *on this very plane*!"

Apologizing

While it's impossible that you've made any mistakes since acquiring this book, your life prior to owning this book was, by definition, one long mistake. Atone for this and other misdeeds committed by your old self by following these five steps:

STEP 1. ADMIT YOUR MISTAKE: This is the hardest part. Look yourself in the mirror, and after you're done complimenting your own appearance, write "I was wrong," on a scrap of paper that you quickly swallow.

STEP 2. EXPRESS REGRET: Track down the person you've wronged, burst into their home or place of business, grab them by the lapels, and shout, "*This is an apology!*" into their eyes as loudly as you can.

STEP 3. DEMAND FORGIVENESS: Present your target with a binding contract absolving you of all legal, moral, and karmic responsibility for your past and future transgressions.

How to Accept an Apology

**Say, "I forgive you,"
with grace, good humor,
and a secret desire
for revenge at any cost.**

STEP 4. CALL IN A FAVOR: Now that your relationship is healed, they owe you, and big time. Refuse to leave until they knit you a special forgiveness hat or admit that the real mistake was making you feel bad enough to apologize in the first place.

STEP 5. MOVE ON: Or, better yet, insist that *they* move, because it is unacceptable to live in the same city as someone who knows you've made a mistake. Have a second apology prepared to make it clear that whatever day they're moving, you're too busy to help.

MAKE AMENDS
TO KEEP NEIGHBORHOOD FRIENDS

**IF YOU'VE MADE ANY OF THE FOLLOWING
COMMON ERRORS, MAKE IT UP TO YOUR NEIGHBORS
WITH THESE EQUIVALENT AMENDS:**

If You Dent Their Driver's Side Door	Dent their passenger's side door for visual balance.
If You Hit a Golf Ball Through Their Window	Replace it. That's right—get yourself a new golf ball.
If You Promise, Then Forget, to Water Their Houseplants	Give them a gift that doesn't need water to survive—a dog.
If You Accidentally Publish a Philosophical Treatise Disproving Their Religious Beliefs	A fruit basket.
If a Tree from Your Property Falls and Crushes Their House	Go over there and soberly confess, "I'm sorry . . . but you owe me a new tree."

Archery

Competitive archers know that the sport is more than just a test of aim. It's a test of will—the will to aim archery equipment correctly. Hit the bull's-eye every time with these steps:

STEP 1. BUILD YOUR OWN EQUIPMENT: Carve an ultralight bow from a single piece of ivory and craft your own arrows by gluing feathers onto a set of steak knives.

STEP 2. IMAGINE VICTORY: Visualize success by imagining the bull's-eye as a charging rhinoceros or a vision of your diabolical twin cousin, ready to strike first.

STEP 3. CONTROL YOUR BREATH: Even the slightest exhalation will cause your arrow to fly wildly off course and into a crowd of your supporters.

STEP 4. READY YOUR AIM: The Earth rotates at 460 meters per second, so you'll want to aim at least a dozen feet to the right of your target (or left, if you are in the Southern Hemisphere).

STEP 5. REMEMBER THE THREE P'S: They are Poise, Precision, and Phobia of losing.

STEP 6. FIRE AWAY: Forgo the notoriously difficult-to-use bowstring and just throw your arrow as hard as you can.

ZENO'S PARADOX

Because a moving arrow must reside in a specific location in space at a given time, Greek paradoxist Zeno proved that movement was impossible. Test his theory by shooting arrows at friends and furniture.

UNDERSTANDING THE ARCHERY TARGET

GOLD The bull's-eye is colored gold, though since 2005 the center target has been made of colored paper as opposed to an actual bull's-eye.

RED The next concentric circle symbolizes the anger of your archery coach at coming so close yet still essentially failing.

BLUE Is worth the same number of points as just shooting an arrow directly into the sky (none).

BLACK Hitting the black ring activates the tiebreaker singing competition.

WHITE If you hit the outermost area of the target, congratulations! The judges will reward your indomitable spirit of nonconformity with an ultravaluable medal made up of the most precious element of all—oxygen.

Bird Watching

Bird watching, or "birding," as experts mistakenly call it, requires all the patience and prowess of hunting, but none of the troubling, fantastic violence or proof that you accomplished anything. Employ this avian advice to spot every bird in existence:

▶ Start by spotting common species like pigeons or dogs (not technically birds, but great practice for looking at things).

▶ Upgrade to professional binoculars—ones that aren't made by holding your rolled-up hands up to your eyes.

▶ Stake out the birds' favorite locations, such as a leafy glen, an exotic pet store, or the sky.

▶ To draw birds to your location, imitate the most alluring bird-call of all: "A hiker dropped most of a muffin" in bird language.

▶ Finally, carry out the experiment that science is too prudish to perform: Release a mason jar of bees to prove that the birds will have sex with them.

TWO BIRDS WITH ONE STONE

Conservationists frown upon crushing any number of birds with rocks, no matter how few rocks you use.

RARE BIRDS FOR THE *ELITE BIRD WATCHER*

Spotting these three rarest birds represents the pinnacle of bird watching:

BALD EAGLE

BALD? You bet.

CONSERVATION STATUS: Endangered But Unafraid

NATURAL HABITAT: In front of waving American flag

HOW TO SPOT: Hum "The Star-Spangled Banner" in front of Mount Rushmore and hold your arm aloft—an eagle will land on it.

☐ SEEN IT

PREHISTORIC MYSTERY . . . SOLVED

Dinosaurs didn't go extinct, they evolved into birds,
which is kind of like if a roller coaster evolved into a library book.

THE ASH-SPECKLED PARTRIDGE

FAVORITE FOOD: Ferns

FAVORITE HABITAT: Gully

FAVORITE MOVIE: *Fern Gully*

HOW TO SPOT: Is *Fern Gully* finally on Netflix?

☐ SEEN IT

FLAMINGO

DANGEROUSNESS LEVEL: 9

HUNTING TECHNIQUE: Appear adorable and flightless—then strangle you with their graceful necks and fly away into the night.

WILL ANYONE BELIEVE YOU? Of course not!

HOW TO SPOT: If you see one, you're already dead.

☐ SEEN IT

Chess

Every battlefield commander, groundbreaking computer scientist, or promising wunderkind turned filth-covered former prodigy has mastered this game of cerebral strategy. Become a grandmaster by employing these tabletop tactics:

STEP 1. THE OPENING GAMBIT Confuse and disarm your opponent by employing a move he'll never expect—pushing an entire row of pieces forward with a hockey stick.

STEP 2. CONTROL THE CENTER Dominate the board, but remember it's considered bad form to move a piece onto a square that already has one of your opponent's pieces on it.

STEP 3. CAPTURE THE QUEEN Disguise the other player's most powerful piece as your own by deftly dipping it into a can of paint while your distracted opponent is foolishly planning several moves ahead.

STEP 4. RISK IT ALL Throw out strategy and embrace the crazed violence that wins all wars: forced-marching your pawns forward and executing your bishops to prove that faith is no armor.

STEP 5. CHECKMATE It's good practice to outmaneuver your opponent until you capture their king, but don't forget that the first player to shout "Checkmate!" at any point during the game automatically wins.

STEAL from the MASTERS

By analyzing the pieces and positions of chess's most momentous matches you can guarantee checkmate for any strategic scenario:

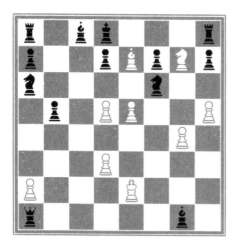

Adolf Anderssen–Lionel Kieseritzky, "The Immortal Game," 1851

WINNING STRATEGY: Anderssen sacrificed both of his rooks, a bishop, and his queen before making the ultimate sacrifice—wagering the life of his son on the match to show he wasn't messing around.

Boris Spassky–David Bronstein,
"The Blue Bird Game," 1960

WINNING STRATEGY:
Surrounded on all sides,
Spassky convinced the
opposing knights to turn on
each other by accusing one
of them of secretly harboring
anti-Soviet sentiments.

Deep Blue–Garry Kasparov,
"The Doritos Spicy Nacho
CrunchTime Chess-Off," 1997

WINNING STRATEGY:
During this grueling contest
of man versus machine, sore
loser Kasparov complained
that Deep Blue was allowed
to use Monopoly pieces including a race car that could
zoom all over the board and
a top hat that "turned his
rook evil."

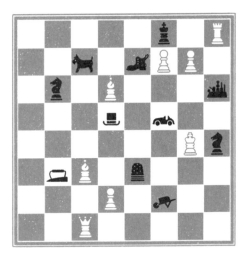

Choosing a Hairstyle

Every successful district attorney, megapastor, and not-yet-disgraced politician wears a hairstyle that telegraphs three things: power, style, and power. Make a statement by giving yourself one of these commanding coifs:

THE LINCOLN

A brimless variation on this stately classic was worn by either Kid or Play of Kid 'n Play.

THE COBRA

Keep jungle predators at bay and charm potential mates into giving it up on the first date. "It" being an open mind to the possibility of a second date.

If You Are Bald

If you're naturally bald, it's a good idea to wear a bald cap anyway so it appears to be by choice.

A COOL SHAPE THAT CONVEYS INDEPENDENT SPIRIT

Show off your individuality with this one-of-a-kind 'do that says, "When it comes to being unique, I . . . JUST DO IT."

THE DOUBLE-DECKER

"Hey, my eyes are up here. *And* up here."

Crime Solving

Once you've reached a certain pinnacle of wealth and success, you have a personal responsibility and legal right to take the law into your own hands. Outwit both criminal masterminds and hardened detectives by collecting the clues to crack the case:

DUST FOR PRINTS This will give you valuable information about the perpetrator's identity, including whether the criminal is a person or a clever, evil dog.

LOOK FOR DNA Comb the crime scene for physical evidence such as strands of hair, an individual skin cell, or the message "Crime Evidence" written on the wall in bloody handprints.

GO UNDERCOVER To earn the trust of local criminals, claim responsibility for a famous crime such as blowing up the *Lusitania* or "Looking this good."

HAVE A CAR CHASE It doesn't matter why or with whom.

GET YOUR MAN The criminal is always the person you least expect . . . meaning, *it was you all along*! Perform a citizen's arrest on yourself and haul your ass down to the precinct. Good work, you'll be going away for a long time.

THE ADVENTURES *of* ALMANAC JACKSON, BOY DETECTIVE

The surest path to solving any crime is having all the facts.
Learn from the example of plucky boy detective Almanac
Jackson, in this excerpt from the 1963 crime classic ALMANAC
JACKSON AND THE CASE OF THE BLAMELESS BULLY:

Landport was much like any other small town—but with one difference: No man, woman, or child ever got away with breaking the law. This was due to the town's Sherlock-in-short-pants, ten-year-old Albert "Almanac" Jackson, the sheriff's son and resident boy sleuth. For only twenty-five cents a day, plus expenses, Almanac, along with his classmate and bodyguard Susie Mathis, could solve any crime, thanks to the mastery of facts that earned Almanac his nickname.

One afternoon, Almanac and Susie had set up shop in the garage when in rushed a most unlikely client. Punch Pilfer was a tough older boy from the wrong side of the tracks, rarely seen without his ratty red jacket. Almanac had often caught him trying to cheat other children in the neighborhood.

"What are you doing here, Punch?" said Almanac.

"I wouldn't be here if I had any other choice, bookworm!" said Punch. "I need to hire you."
"We don't work for bullies," said Susie.

"You're nuts!" said Punch. "I've been accused of a crime I didn't commit. Here, I'll even pay you up front."

Punch handed Almanac a shiny quarter.

"A 1932-S," declared Almanac. "The 'S' means it was minted in San Francisco. OK, what's the case?"

"Old Widow McClatchkey set a strawberry pie on the windowsill to cool and she thinks I stole it, because she heard her bulldog barking. She says that, like a real bull, her bulldog is trained to bark at anything red—like my red jacket!"

Almanac thought for one moment before uttering, "Solution Solved! You can tell Widow McClatchkey you're innocent—*this* time."

HOW DID ALMANAC KNOW?

Almanac explained, "Widow McClatchkey's bulldog, like all dogs, is color-blind to shades of red! There's no way it could've identified you by your red jacket." Susie nodded, and even Punch was impressed. Another case closed.

Just then, Almanac's father's battered police car plowed into the garage. Sheriff Jackson staggered out, hands trembling and slick with blood.

"Almanac, I need you to solve a murder."

"Whose?" asked the boy detective.

". . . My own."

Almanac's father fell face-forward onto the concrete garage floor—dead—blood pooling beneath him, ending Almanac's childhood right then and there.

Visit AlmanacJackson.com to help Almanac solve
"The Case of the Fallen Father!"

Dentist
Appointments

Everyone deserves a winning smile, but there's one person stand-ing in the way: your dentist, the dignity-robbing semi-doctor who's more interested in chastising you than in fixing your teeth. Win your next dental checkup by staying on the orthodontic offensive:

WHEN THE RECEPTIONIST ASKS YOU TO SIGN IN:
This is a trick so they can try to sell you more teeth. Give a fake name and the address of the dentist's rival—a candy store.

WHEN THE HYGIENIST ASKS YOU HOW OFTEN YOU FLOSS:
Answer directly and say, "After every meal," or answer honestly and say, "Never."

WHEN THE DENTIST DISCOVERS A CAVITY:
Reply, "That's not a cavity, it's a spare food hole—but I would be reluctantly willing to let you fill it with free gold."

BRACE YOURSELF . . .
. . . For how cool you'll look with a mouth full of braces.

WHEN THE DENTIST ATTEMPTS TO RENDER YOU UNCONSCIOUS WITH LAUGHING GAS:

Prove the gas isn't lethal by demanding the dentist take a sizable huff first.

WHEN THE DENTIST FINISHES VIOLATING YOUR MOUTH WITH HIS FINGERTIPS AND RAZOR-SHARP IMPLEMENTS:

Now's your chance! Steal a toothbrush with his name and phone number on it and a minitube of bubblegum-flavored toothpaste. This contraband will let you put off your next appointment for at least six months.

HYGIENE *at* HOME

Though most people rely on the dentist, many don't realize you can also clean your teeth at home:

BRUSHING: *Grasp the soft bristles of your toothbrush in your fingertips to comfort your hand while you vigorously scrape the inside of your mouth with the hard plastic end.*

MOUTHWASH: *Swirl it around in your mouth, but don't swallow—spit it back into the bottle to trap your germs.*

TOOTH WHITENING STRIPS: *You can make your own out of Scotch tape, Wite-Out, and the phone number for Poison Control.*

Directing a Blockbuster

The best way to command undue influence over an entire culture is to turn your personal vision of the world into a blockbuster summer movie. Don't let anyone compromise your art or percentage of the profit—make a hit movie on your own with these five steps of Hollywood-style filmmaking:

STEP 1. SCRIPTING: This least important (but for some reason necessary) step of making a movie involves crafting a screenplay so heartfelt and personal that sizzling nudity and dazzling robot attacks spring from the story organically. Rule of thumb: a 90-minute film should take no longer than 90 minutes to write.

STEP 2. CASTING: Obviously you'll be casting yourself, but be sure to take an appropriate role, such as a rogue movie director who has to stop an evil supermodel by falling in love with their even more attractive twin. Consider also giving yourself a small but crucial cameo as entire family of funny fat people.

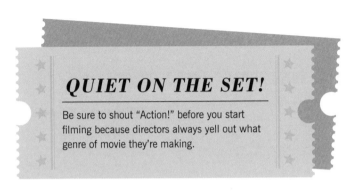

QUIET ON THE SET!

Be sure to shout "Action!" before you start filming because directors always yell out what genre of movie they're making.

STEP 3. DIRECTING: On the first day of shooting, throw your script into a garbage can. Then spend two-thirds of the shoot berating actors and one-third of the shoot pointing a camera at explosions.

STEP 4. COMPOSING THE SCORE, CREATING THE SPECIAL EFFECTS, PAINSTAKINGLY EDITING THE FINAL CUT OF THE FILM: They have computers for this now!

STEP 5. ADVERTISING: This most important step of making a movie involves distributing action-packed trailers and eye-catching posters. Or, you can skip all the other steps and launch an advertising campaign so compelling that people will just mail you their money instead of going to the theater.

BEEF UP YOUR BOX OFFICE

★ ★ ★ ★ ★ ★ ★ ★ ★ ★ ★ ★ ★ ★ ★ ★ ★ ★ ★ ★

To attract record-breaking audiences on your film's
opening weekend, be sure to include these elements
shared by the highest-grossing films in history:

Car chases

. . . .

★ ★ ★ **A hip-hop hedgehog** ★ ★ ★

. . . .

**A gruff protagonist who butts heads—but
later falls in love with—a beautiful, strong-
willed canister of microfilm**

. . . .

★ ★ ★ **The *Star Wars* music** ★ ★ ★

. . . .

**Technologically advanced aliens who forgot
about one thing: *the human spirit***

. . . .

**A suspenseful part where you don't know
what's going to happen**

. . . .

**A boring part at the end that's just a list
of scrolling names for some reason**

. . . .

★ ★ ★ **Dracula?** ★ ★ ★

OSCAR BAIT

Easily snag an Academy Award by setting your film
in a dramatic time period like World War II
or an alternate universe where dinosaurs won World War II.

Door-to-Door Salesmanship

With fewer and fewer salesmen knocking on doors nationwide, you're sure to make a killing in this lucrative, wide-open field— if you can master the art of the sell. Tailor your look and pattern your patter after this ideal door-to-door salesman:

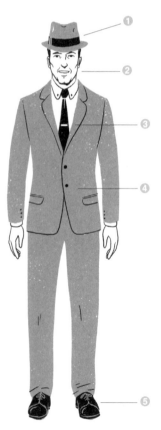

1 **FEDORA:** It's fashion shorthand for "I can't be a murderer, I'm dressed too nicely."

2 **WINNING SMILE:** In the face of frequent rejection, you must turn your scowl inside-out into a mask of confidence.

3 **SILVER TIEPIN:** Be sure to mention that it was awarded for "Best Use of a Professional Accolade in Order to Project an Image of Success."

4 **PAUNCH:** Not fat, not flat.

5 **GLEAMING WINGTIPS:** Do anything to get your foot in the door, up-to and including taking off your shoe and throwing it into the house. They'll have to let you in, then!

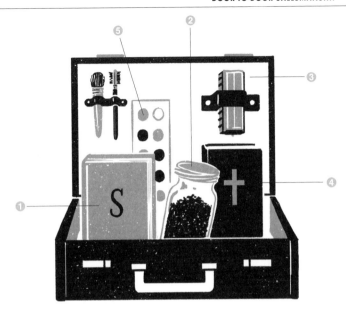

① COMPLIMENTARY ENCYCLOPEDIA VOLUME:
Get them hooked with the most exciting volume, S—Sex,
Second World War, and Swear Words.

**② JAR OF DIRT TO POUR ON CARPET FOR VACUUM
CLEANER DEMONSTRATION:** Even if you're not selling
vacuum cleaners, they'll appreciate all the free dirt.

③ 10-CENT HARMONICA: You can sell it for thousands by
convincing uncultured customers it's a grand piano.

④ BIBLE: "Buy today and get an additional eleventh command-
ment for free!"

⑤ MAKEUP SAMPLES: Use them to disguise yourself if the
lady of the house accidentally slips and dies and you become
wanted for murder.

GETTING YOUR FOOT IN THE DOOR

For some reason, many people have trepidation about letting a stranger into their home. Counter these common objections so you can share your wares:

"My spouse makes all the purchasing decisions for our home"

"Don't think of it as a purchase—think of it as two new friends giving each other gifts to celebrate Salesman's Day."

"I just bought a brand-new [whatever you're selling]"

"Then maybe I can interest you in this vintage model with classic styling and timeless, inferior features."

"My kids are always spilling grape juice on the carpet, but surely there's no miracle product that can provide an astonishing deep clean!"

"Stop blaming all your problems on your children and buy this."

Dreaming

Dreams are a subconscious swirl of your innermost hopes, anxieties, and brilliant inventions that you'll never remember. Decode your dreams' symbolic imagery to turn unconscious guidance into waking-world advantages:

DREAM SYMBOL: You're flying.

WHAT IT MEANS: You're ready for success in your personal and professional endeavors.

WHAT TO DO: Fly into the office tomorrow on a cloud of optimism. Metaphorically tackle a big project and literally tackle your office crush to get their attention.

DREAM SYMBOL: You're naked in public.

WHAT IT MEANS: You're concealing a shameful secret.

WHAT TO DO: Get it off your chest by confessing to a trusted confidant such as a clergy member, butler who you intend to be buried with, or anonymous Internet blog that you cleverly sign with just your initials and home address.

DREAM SYMBOL: Reuniting with a lost love.

WHAT IT MEANS: You're still pining for your ex.

WHAT TO DO: When you wake up, send your ex a clear, direct signal of your intentions that cannot be misinterpreted—a text message that says, "Hey."

DREAM SYMBOL: You're in your house, but it's not exactly your house, but it is your house.

WHAT IT MEANS: That is messed up, man. Normal people don't dream about stuff like that.

WHAT TO DO: Move into a new place with only one room, ideally a hospital for people who experience such disturbing, abnormal nightmares.

DREAM SYMBOL: You're being chased.

WHAT IT MEANS: Like all living things, you're scared of being chased.

WHAT TO DO: Don't let your dream chase you—chase your dream! That is, the dream of staying up for days on end to avoid returning to your subconscious prison of baffling nighttime hallucinations.

IF YOU DREAM OF EATING THE WORLD'S LARGEST MARSHMALLOW . . .

. . . And you wake up to find that your pillow is missing, these are two separate problems.

PROPHETIC DREAMS

Sometimes dreams foretell things to come. Find out what your future holds if you dream about:

FINDING A WINNING LOTTERY TICKET: You will soon receive a large sum of money.

THE WIND RUSHES PAST YOU AS YOU ARE PERPETUALLY FALLING: Expect a "wind fall" . . . of money.

YOUR SPOUSE IS JUST A SHADOW AND EVERY TIME YOU REACH OUT TO TOUCH THEIR FACE YOUR HAND IS SWALLOWED BY THE DARKNESS: Money!

NEVER WAKE A SLEEPWALKER.

This is because if they are dreaming you're about to wake them up, they'll lose the ability to tell which world is reality.

Exterminating Pests

As a human being, you are granted dominion over all animals and people who are smaller than you, especially in your own home. Exert your primacy over these lesser beings who bring in filth, disease, and little poops that look deceptively like delicious Raisinets by using these pest control protocols:

RATS To rid your home of rats, bring in their natural predator—a cat. Then, when all the rats are taken care of, bring in the cat's natural predator—a box of cat poison.

COCKROACHES Stepping on even one cockroach will send its comrades a clear message: "This psychopath isn't screwing around! We must stop bothering the human race forever."

SILVERFISH Leave them be. Six months from now, these drain-dwelling creepers will have metamorphosed into much more valuable goldfish.

HAUNTING MEMORIES
STEP 1: Fumigate your brain by filling a humidifier with whiskey.
STEP 2: Burn down any rooms you have cried in.

SATAN, IN THE FORM OF CHUCK BERRY RECORDS
Don't throw them in a fire, that's where Satan is most comfortable! The safest way to rid your home of the King of Tricks is never to indulge in the pleasures of music.

the
PERFECT TRAP

Animals are constantly evolving to become
more intelligent, but you can vanquish all vermin
with these inescapable traps:

MOUSETRAP: Bait the trap with something no mouse can
resist—a casting notice for *Fievel 3: Two More Until Five-el?*

ROACH MOTEL: Paralyze roaches with existential dread by
reading them *The Metamorphosis* backward.

FLYPAPER: Hit the fly with a rolled up paper.

**DO YOU REALLY SWALLOW SEVEN SPIDERS
EVERY YEAR?**

Yes, but they provide the recommended dosage of things
that are terrifying to have inside you.

Eye Exam

Even if you need glasses, there's no reason to admit weakness and fail your eye exam. Avoid prescription eyewear (the crutches of the face) and effortlessly ace this ocular obstacle by memorizing the standard Snellen chart, printed below:

E

V E

R Y O

N E D I E

S A L O N E

L I F E I S M E

A N I N G L E S S *

*Even many patients with 20/20 vision will not allow themselves to see this message.

SIGHTLESS SURVIVAL

If your eyesight is failing, you can still navigate society despite not actually being able to see it.

BEHIND THE WHEEL: If you see a red sign with eight sides, it means, "STOP trying to read this sign and get to where you're going as fast as you can."

ON THE HOME FRONT: It doesn't matter if you can no longer spot the difference between the stove and the refrigerator—placing raw meat into either of these appliances for 45 minutes will make it safe and delicious to eat.

AT THE MOVIES: Who cares if you can't see the screen? Just focus on the deafening explosions, which are the only good parts of movies anyway.

HIPPOCRATIC HYPOCRITES

Optometrists know that the eyes are the most sensitive parts of your body, which is why they think nothing of wrenching them open with metal hooks and shooting lasers into them.

fig. 1A

fig. 1B

fig. 1C

BENEFITS OF BLINDNESS

*Sacrificing your sight grants you the eternal companionship
of a seeing eye dog, who will use animal language to recruit
a helpful smelling nose hawk and an empathy squid.*

Faking Your Own Death

Now that you've won at everything in life, seal your legend by orchestrating a spectacular death—then surviving it. Ensure that your lifetime of unbelievable success enters the history books by disappearing without a trace so you can tell future generations how great you were.

GET OFF THE GRID: Erase all evidence of your current life—burn your library card, write the word *dead* on your birth certificate in red marker, and bake your passport into a pie to feed to the very family you plan to abandon.

MAKE A MEMORABLE EXIT: Stage one of the following massively unforgettable death scenarios:

> **NEWSWORTHY:** *Drive a classic Corvette off of a famous covered bridge and right into the last surviving manatee mating with the last surviving panda.*

> **CURSED:** *Pretend to set off on a life-risking expedition into a mummy's pyramid built atop an ancient Egyptian burial ground.*

> **INSPIRING:** *Leave a pile of your clothes on the ground next to a torn piece of paper that says "Raptured."*

MEET THE NEW YOU

**After you've faked your own death,
take this opportunity to reinvent yourself as:**

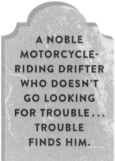

A NOBLE
MOTORCYCLE-
RIDING DRIFTER
WHO DOESN'T
GO LOOKING
FOR TROUBLE...
TROUBLE
FINDS HIM.

A
CONGRESSMAN

(IF YOU'RE
ALREADY A
CONGRESSMAN,
BECOME *TWO*
CONGRESSMEN.)

SHAQ

SCOPE OUT YOUR FUNERAL: Attend your own memorial service. Claim to be your own ghost and berate anyone who isn't crying hard enough.

EMBRACE YOUR FREEDOM: Live without consequence, morals, or traditional human dignity. Make so many mistakes barreling through your new life that the only way to pick yourself up is to start this book again from the beginning. We're sorry. You're welcome.

Fighting a House Fire

Since time immemorial, fire has been jealous of mankind's stranglehold on precious oxygen resources. Should a fire break into your home and threaten your family, you can fully extinguish the flaming foe with these firefighting methods:

▸ At the first sign of smoke, stop what you're doing, drop to the ground, and roll the fire into a carpet so you can whack it with a rolled-up magazine.

▸ Return to the scene of the fire prepared with an oxygen mask, *Scream* mask, or fishbowl helmet filled with fireproof water.

▸ Now, fight the fire with fire by throwing a handful of matches into the flames to burn the fire down.

▸ If the fire continues to rage unabated, try reasoning with it by pointing out other, nicer homes nearby that it would enjoy burning more.

▸ You can never fully extinguish any fire. Instead, fan it down to a manageable size, scoop it up into a cardboard box, and hide it safely away in a closet where it can never hurt anyone.

FIRE AND WATER DON'T MIX

Fire, like its cousin electricity, is easily conducted
by water and will spread faster if you get it wet.

Fistfights

The average adult gets into one to three fights a year, with the exception of disciplined clergymen and people who aren't really living their lives to the fullest. Whether defending yourself against a barroom blowhard or finally settling the question of free will versus determinism like men, finish first in any fight with this knock-out knowledge:

SPOT TROUBLE Be aware of possible aggressors who exhibit any of the following brawl-baiting signs: scowling, looking at you too much (or not enough), or currently punching you.

DEFUSE THE SITUATION Say, "Hey, man, we're cool," *even if you're not cool.*

TAKE THE HIT If you can't dodge an assailant's punch, rob his fist of its precious kinetic energy by absorbing it with your face.

THE PERFECT PUNCH To retaliate, curl your fingers into a tight fist, but don't aim your punch where your opponent *is*, aim where he's going to be—the hospital.

FINISH THE JOB Pivot forward on your nondominant foot and plant a decisive wallop on one of these pressure points:

1. Jugular
2. Government-issued tracking chip implanted by "flu shots"
3. Funny bone
4. One-touch death spot
5. Bowl of organs
6. Balls (on a lady they are on the inside and called "ovaries")
7. Elbow, Jr.
8. Shin (the genitals of the leg)

BE THE BIGGER PERSON Help your vanquished adversary to his feet, offer to buy the next round, and agree to work together to tackle the real problem—mankind's thirst for violence.

FEROCIOUS FIGHTING STYLES

Before entering combat, create an unstoppable move set by training in an array of historical fighting styles:

GENTLEMEN'S FISTICUFFS

SIGNATURE MOVE: **THE HANDLEBAR HAYMAKER**

Remove your waistcoat and sock your opponent so hard that he tumbles off the dock you're standing on and onto a steamship bound for the Orient.

OKINAWAN GOJU RYU

SIGNATURE MOVE: **THE CRANE KICK**

Embody the grace and poise of the noble crane to kick your opponent in the face as hard as you can.

JAILHOUSE ROCK (A.K.A., FIFTY-TWO HAND BLOCKS)

SIGNATURE MOVE: **THE LOCKDOWN**

Disable jailhouse opponents by recounting an anecdote from their victims' lives in order to cripple them with guilt.

YOU WOULDN'T HIT A GUY WITH GLASSES

The same courtesy extends to the opposite, handsome people.

COMBAT CATCHPHRASES

AFTER PHYSICALLY DISABLING AN AGGRESSOR,
BREAK HIS SPIRIT WITH A CLASSY CATCHPHRASE, SUCH AS:

"...and stay down."

"I love being a turtle."

"I'm the RoboCop ... of the South."

"The third rule of Fight Club? Die hard ... with a vengeance."

FOXY BOXING

SIGNATURE MOVE: **THE VOLCANO**

Oh, no! You got massage oil on *both* of you!

CONSCIENTIOUS OBJECTION

SIGNATURE MOVE: **THE ATTICUS FINCH**

Demonstrate that you're above the fray by handling your conflicts in a court of law but keep everybody on their toes by shooting a dog in the head from super far away.

CLOSE QUARTERS COMBAT (CQC)

SIGNATURE MOVE: **THE EQUALIZER**

If an attacker draws a knife, disarm him with an easy smile and the peacemaking Bible verse, "Let us *not* get ready to rumble."

Genealogy

It's imperative to keep your friends close, your enemies closer, and your family members so close that they have to say "Yes" when you ask to borrow money or an organ. Keep tabs on the potential allies, and the even more potential enemies, that populate your family tree by completing this universal genealogical chart:

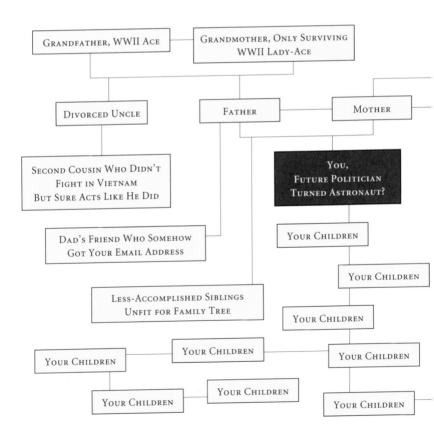

ADAM AND EVE

GREAT-GRANDFATHER, ARCHDUKE OF _____

GREAT-GRANDMOTHER, COUNTESS-TURNED-SILENT-FILM-ACTRESS TURNED-GREAT-GRANDMOTHER

CLEOPATRA (ACCORDING TO FORTUNE TELLER YOUR MOM MET AT THE RENAISSANCE FAIRE)

EINSTEIN—THAT'S RIGHT, JAZZ GUITARIST FREDDY EINSTEIN

GRANDFATHER, ALSO FOUGHT IN WWII BUT WON'T SAY FOR WHO

STEP-GRANDMOTHER, LONG-LOST MEMBER OF RUSSIAN ROYAL FAMILY BUT DOESN'T MAKE A BIG FUSS OVER IT

REAL FATHER WHO PROBABLY DIDN'T HAVE TIME FOR YOU BECAUSE HE WAS A FAMOUS GLOBETROTTING BULLFIGHTER

MOM'S SISTER WHO SHE DOESN'T TALK TO

WEIRD UNCLE

AUNT

YOUR FAMILY'S OWN REAL-LIFE COUSIN OLIVER

COOL UNCLE

DIABOLICAL TWIN COUSIN

MORE-ACCOMPLISHED SIBLINGS WHO THINK THEY'RE TOO GOOD FOR FAMILY TREE

COUSIN YOU HAVE IN COMMON WITH THE FAMOUS ARQUETTE ACTING DYNASTY

YOUR CHILDREN

YOUR CHILDREN

YOUR CHILDREN

YOUR CHILDREN

YOUR CHILDREN

YOUR CHILDREN

YOUR CHILDREN

YOUR CHILDREN

YOUR CHILDREN

Giving Birth

At some point, every adult will undergo the excruciating miracle of childbirth. Here's a step-by-step guide to expelling a newborn:

STEP 1. **YOUR WATER BREAKS.** Don't panic.

STEP 2. **START PANICKING.** Is your baby OK? Probably . . . *or maybe not!* There's no way to know. Grab an overnight bag containing a list of letters you can combine into baby names and a stuffed bear you can use to scare the baby into submission if it comes out evil.

STEP 3. **COUNT THE CONTRACTIONS.** If your doctor uses more than four contractions (e.g., *can't, don't, shan't*) he (or she!) is obviously uneducated and unqualified to deliver your baby.

STEP 4. **FACE THE PAIN.** You can either cheat by taking a painkilling epidural or experience the full joy of feeling like you're being sheared in half by the lid of a giant soup can.

STEP 5. **BREATHE.** But just once—take a single giant breath and hold it for the duration of labor.

KNOW THE POINTS OF A BABY

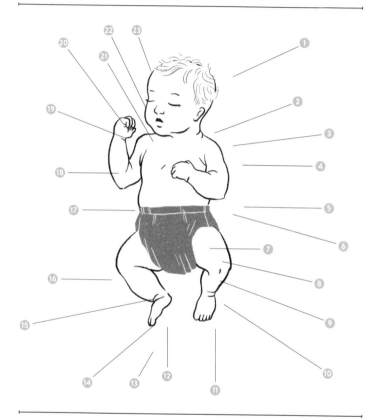

1. Poil
2. Crest
3. Back
4. Withers
5. Elbow
6. Fool's Elbow
7. Loins
8. Thigh
9. Gaskin
10. Hock
11. Cannon
12. Fetlock
13. Pastern
14. Coronet
15. Stifle
16. Knee
17. Dock
18. Croup
19. Grizgrap
20. Bockwinkel
21. Barrel
22. Muzzle
23. Forehead

STEP 6. PUSH. Your baby should slide out gently into the waiting arms of a doctor or a cushiony pile of autumn leaves.

STEP 7. HOLD YOUR BABY FOR THE FIRST TIME. It will be covered in a thin nutrient slime that should not be scraped off until its thirteenth birthday.

The Four Trimesters

Your pregnancy will be divided into four distinct trimesters. Here's what you can expect while you're expecting:

THE FIRST TRIMESTER: You'll experience raging bouts of morning sickness, afternoon illness, and night terrors. You may also crave unusual foods like ice cream smeared across a wooden plank, or a ham carved into your own likeness.

THE SECOND TRIMESTER: You'll begin to show, causing strangers, landlocked sea captains, and nostalgic babies to rub your belly for good luck. Start investing in maternity clothes and a maternity car.

THE THIRD TRIMESTER: Enroll in Lamaze classes, which is French for *the maze.*

THE FOURTH TRIMESTER: You'll want to avoid flying, roller coasters, and go-karts to prevent your child from inheriting your lust for danger.

Incapacitating Attackers Using Only this Book

Reading this book in public will make you a target for lawbreakers seeking to filch the riches you'll inevitably garner from following its advice. Defend your person by using this book in the manner it was intended—as a deadly weapon:

fig. 1

COLLARBONE CRUSH

Swing the book's sturdy spine down upon your attacker's collarbone, fracturing it. Be careful, as their now-higher medical bills may drive them to rob you even more.

fig. 2

PUNCH PROTECTOR

Grip the edges of the book tightly to form a shield for blocking incoming punches, elbow strikes, or scary looks.

fig. 3

SWINGING SLICE

Graze your attacker with the razor-sharp edges of the book's pages to inflict stinging paper cuts that are relatively harmless but disproportionately painful.

fig. 4

REHABILITATING RECITATION

Disarm your opponent with the most effective weapon of all—knowledge—instantly causing your attacker to abandon a life of crime for a life of introspection.

SAVING LIVES USING ONLY THIS BOOK

Keep this bulletproof* book in your front shirt pocket at all times.

Only book's knowledge is bulletproof.

Juggling Work and Family

There's no need to put your career on the back burner just to teach your children how to read or fear the correct god—you can have it all! When facing the following work/family dilemmas, achieve triumph in both the homestead and the workstead with these win-win solutions:

DILEMMA ▶ You're stuck late at the office on the night of your son's holiday pageant.

SOLUTION ★ Compromise by bringing your laptop to the performance. You can finish your work while jotting down harsh but valid criticisms to improve your son's embarrassingly amateurish performance.

DILEMMA ▶ Your family requires a hot, healthy, and wholesome dinner, but you're running late due to a conference call in another time zone.

SOLUTION ★ There's no substitute for a home-cooked meal prepared with love—except for the stunningly delicious array of choices offered by your neighborhood fast-food restaurants. They're quick, tasty, and infused with a full week's worth of life-giving sodium.

FREE DAY CARE

The state provides working parents with a free babysitting service known as "school."

DILEMMA ▶ You find a joint in your teenager's sock drawer right before the most important meeting of your life.

SOLUTION ★ Put your teen through the ultimate punishment—watching their parent subject themselves to the horrors of drug use. Then rush over to your meeting to wow the boss with your new laid-back attitude and mind-blowing ideas.

DILEMMA ▶ You keep getting passed over for a promotion and your eldest daughter is dating some cool, rebellious loser.

SOLUTION ★ Secure your daughter's happiness, as well as your place in the company's future, by arranging a marriage between her and the guy who fixes the printer.

DILEMMA ▶ Your boss introduces you to the company's latest hire and your hotshot new business rival, *your own spouse!?*

SOLUTION ★ No one ever said you could have it all; quit your family and divorce your job. The settlement and severance will let you learn how to juggle what really matters: your newfound independent wealth and parade of noncommittal sex partners.

WORKPLACE-INSPIRED BABY NAMES

The ultimate synthesis of work and family is to bless your progeny with one of these workplace-inspired baby names:

TONER

EXCEL

JUNIOR

(short for "Junior Vice-President")

WARREN BUFFETT

CASH

Losing Gracefully

By even reading the opening words of this chapter, you have already allowed defeat into your heart. Throw the book out of the window of your car—when you're ready, the book will find you again.

Losing Thirty Pounds in Thirty Days

In the battle for fitness, you have only one enemy—no, not the ease and glamour of a sedentary lifestyle—it's your mind. But you also have a second enemy—your body. Follow this thirty-day regimen to slim down and slay sloth:

DAY 1	DAY 2	DAY 3
REWARD DAY Take the day off from exercising and indulge in sweets.	**GET SERIOUS** About rewarding yourself with more sweets and relaxation.	**EXERCISE** ...your free will by taking a day to pig out and catch your breath.

DAY 8	DAY 9	DAY 10
WALK TO WORK If it's too far to walk, walk as far as you can, then call in sick and fall asleep where you stand.	**PUMP SOME IRON** Seal off your pants cuffs with rubber bands and fill your pants with heavy ball bearings for a secret workout all day.	**TAKE A DIP** If you can't swim, that's OK—flailing wildly is terrific exercise.

MOTIVATIONAL MANTRAS

Keep yourself motivated throughout the month with any of these confidence-boosting affirmations:

"Fit mind. Fit body. Fit into my children's clothes."

"Exercise is 90% perspiration, 10% remembering catchy slogans."

"The Little Engine That Could didn't do whatever it was that *he* did by being a fat sack of crap."

DAY 4	DAY 5	DAY 6	DAY 7
SHAME DAY You haven't even started getting in shape! Take today to wallow in self-pity in front of the TV.	**HYDRATE** Wine has water in it, right?	**HANGOVER DAY** Sleep has exercise in it, right?	**STOCK UP** Purchase fitness essentials such as barbells of every increment, a canister of bee pollen, a T-shirt that says "Exercise," and a bathtub full of gravy to ignore.

DAY 11	DAY 12	DAY 13	DAY 14
YOM KIPPUR	**BUILD MUSCLE** ...with traditional exercises like the bench press, in which you walk up to a park bench and impress the people sitting on it by flexing your biceps.	**DEMONSTRATE WILLPOWER** Heartily season your bathtub full of gravy just to prove that you can make it as delicious as it could possibly be and still not taste even a single drop.	**UPGRADE YOUR GEAR** Challenge yourself with as-seen-on-TV fitness products such as the Climb 'N' Rock, the AbShockeress, and the GluteGaloot.

DAY 15

DO

DAY 16

NOT

DAY 17

EAT

DAY 22

SWEAT IT OUT

Wrap yourself tightly in garbage bags to rid your body of the water weight that's weighing you down and preventing your kidneys from turning into ash.

DAY 23

BEGIN CRASH DIET

It's getting late. Try a controversial fad diet such as the Master Cleanse, the Cabbage Soup Diet, or the Eat Anything You Want Out of the Trash Diet.

DAY 24

BREATHE DEEP

Cut down on bloating by breathing only through your ears.

DAY 29

SHAVE OFF A FEW

The average person is carrying around five pounds of body hair.

DAY 30

Congratulations! Now that you've sculpted a healthy new you, it's safe to eat heaping platefuls of whatever you want, as long as it's garnished with a single radish.

DAY 18	DAY 19	DAY 20	DAY 21
DURING	**THIS**	**WEEK**	

DAY 25	DAY 26	DAY 27	DAY 28
EMBRACE YOUR SPIRIT ANIMAL If your spirit animal is a Twinkie, you can still give it kisses, but closed-mouth only.	**THE HARDEST EXERCISE OF ALL** Explain to your kids that the cat drowned in the bathtub full of gravy.	**SNACK ON SUPERFOODS** Even just a handful of acai berries will let you see through walls and lies.	**CHEAT DAY** You earned it— go ahead and cheat on your spouse.

FOLLOW THE FOOD PYRAMID

These guidelines for nutritious eating explain that any food is healthy if you cut it into the shape of a pyramid.

The Lottery

Most people believe that, like getting hit by lightning, winning the lottery is something that can only happen to them once a year. Hit the jackpot every time with these mathematical formulas for choosing your lucky numbers:

FORMULA 1

(Birth date of your firstborn child) − (Number of times they've disappointed you) =

FORMULA 2

(Number of nights you've spent in jail) ÷ (Number of crimes you intend to commit after you become so wealthy that human laws are beneath you) =

FORMULA 3

(Your home address) + (Your passport ID number) + (Your ATM pin) + (A tricky zero at the end so the rube behind the counter doesn't realize he has all your personal information) =

FORMULA 4

(Number of instances of the word Guv'nor in the first sixteen pages of *Pygmalion*) × (Number of hats you're currently wearing) =

MORE VALUABLE THAN GOLD

Reinvest your lottery winnings in millet seed. When society collapses, this hearty grain can be poured into a tube sock to make a homemade blackjack.

FORMULA 5

(The sexiest number, 69)   +   (Length of time, in minutes, you laughed after reading "69")   =

FORMULA 6

(Dial a random phone number and if the person on the other end sounds nice)   =   Play that number immediately.

TRUE WEALTH

Whoever said, "Money can't buy happiness" was obviously a rich person lying to a crowd of poor people.

Love

There are winners and losers in love. When you're enamored of another person, your judgment becomes cloudy, rendering you dangerously emotional. Stay on top in your relationship by looking for these signals that your "partner" is plotting something:

IF THEY ASK YOU ON A DATE

This is a desperate ploy to gain insight into your personal weaknesses. Cunningly accept, then use the opportunity to gather intel about their own interests and family history.

IF YOU CATCH THEM WATCHING YOU SLEEP

Reach out and bring them close to your chest as you sleep, so they can't escape, or grab a knife.

IF THEY SAY, "I DO"

This a trick to throw you off guard.
In a calculated act of verbal judo, deflect their "I do," by repeating it back at them.

BLIND DATE BLUNDER

If you can't help audibly sighing in disappointment when you see your blind date, cover up your rudeness by saying "[Sigh] . . .ns is the most cohesive M. Night Shyamalan movie. Great to meet you."

IF THEIR HAND GENTLY CLASPS YOURS WHILE WATCHING YOUR DAUGHTER TAKE HER FIRST STEPS

Check to see if their palm is lined with thumbtacks.

IF YOU'VE ENTERED YOUR TWILIGHT YEARS TOGETHER, ROCKING ON THE PORCH AND TAKING IN SUNSETS

Now is the time to strike—die unexpectedly in their arms leaving them nothing but a lifetime of precious memories and a small army of supportive grandchildren.

MAKE SURE THEY'RE THE ONE

Go ahead and sleep with a bunch of other people. If you feel bad about it, you've found your soul mate.

Maintaining the Illusion of Santa Claus's Existence

[NOTE: If you currently believe in Santa—and why wouldn't you!—please skip to the next chapter. This one is just for Mommies and Daddies.]

No matter which religion you're indoctrinating your children into, instilling a healthy fear of and reverence for Santa Claus will allow you to manipulate your offspring into behaving well throughout the year. Become a master of yuletide deception with these pretense-perpetuating tips:

INTRODUCE THE CONCEPT OF SANTA BY AGE TWO

He's a magical toymaker who rewards good children and is God's brother.

HAVE YOUR CHILDREN WRITE LETTERS TO SANTA

Then send a reply from a North Pole address explaining that while Santa's workshop is magical, every child in your family has a strict two toy limit on how much magic they can receive this year.

EVERY COUPLE OF YEARS, GIVE EVERYONE COAL FOR CHRISTMAS

Because a loving parent would never do such a thing, but a vindictive polar demigod would have no such compunction.

ON CHRISTMAS MORNING, DRESS UP AS SANTA

This will hammer home the point that while Santa will always be there for your kids, one of their parents may be conspicuously absent for a few important holidays.

Clausible Deniability

If your children raise these common objections to
Santa's existence, counter with the provided retorts:

"How can Santa visit every house in one night?"

"Santa disregards large swaths of the planet inhabited by heathens,
and his moral standards are so high that he considers even
many children who believe in him to be irredeemably corrupt."

"How can Santa know if I've been bad or good
when he lives all the way at the north pole?"

"Do you think *I* want to get in trouble?
I tell him everything you're doing!"

"Isn't Santa Claus just a marketing tool that retailers use to
reduce familial love to a series of capitalistic transactions?"

"No. Here, take this present . . ."

Mastering Your Memory

The world's most formidable intellects can call forth an encyclopedia's worth of facts at a moment's notice. The following mnemonics will cram your cranium with crucial details that give you the edge at your next bar trivia night or UN General Assembly meeting:

THE MUSICAL SCALE

(E, G, B, D, F):

Every Good Boy Decries Fascism.

THE SOLAR SYSTEM

(MERCURY, VENUS, EARTH, MARS, JUPITER, SATURN, URANUS, NEPTUNE, PLUTO):

My Very Educated Mother Just Severed Uncle Nathan's Perineum.

THE GREAT LAKES

(H.O.U.S.E.):

Huron, Ontario, Unnerving lake-shaped-like-human-face (formerly Lake Michigan), Superior, Erie.

THE LENGTHS OF THE MONTHS

Thirty days hath September / And the rest I can't remember.

THE FIRST FIVE EMPERORS OF ROME

(AUGUSTUS, TIBERIUS, CALIGULA, CLAUDIUS, NERO):

"Alan Thicke's Cool!" Claims Nobody.

DAYLIGHT SAVING TIME

Spring forward, Fall forward 23 hours.

THE BOOKS OF THE OLD TESTAMENT

(GENESIS, EXODUS, LEVITICUS, NUMBERS, DEUTERONOMY):

God's Existence Lamentably Now Doubtful.

THE FIVE OCEANS

(ATLANTIC, ARCTIC, PACIFIC, SOUTHERN, INDIAN):

Amusing Acronyms Postpone Sailors' Insanity.

COLORS OF THE VISIBLE SPECTRUM

(RED, ORANGE, YELLOW, GREEN, BLUE, INDIGO, VIOLET):

You don't have to memorize these, because you can see them.

MNEMONIC TO MEMORIZING THIS LIST OF MNEMONICS

(GREAT LAKES, EMPERORS, COLORS, OCEANS, SOLAR SYSTEM, MONTHS, MUSICAL SCALE, DAYLIGHT SAVING, OLD TESTAMENT):

Google-Equipped Computers or Smartphones Make Memorizing Data Obsolete.

Mourning

Whether you are mourning the loss of a beloved fiancé, pet turtle, or pet turtle's beloved fiancé, the five stages of grief are universal. Win at mourning by blasting through these burdensome emotions as quickly as possible, so you can get back to focusing on the life that matters—your own:

STAGE 1.
DENIAL

TELL YOURSELF: "Good-looking people can't die."

Cheat death a little bit every day by drinking ten glasses of alkaline water, swallowing 150 vitamins, and refusing to be an organ donor.

STAGE 2.
ANGER

TELL YOURSELF: "Go to hell, Death!"

Anger is just one letter away from *danger*. Taunt the Grim Reaper with fate-defying stunts such as bungee jumping or breaking a mirror by throwing a black cat at it.

STAGE 3.
BARGAINING

TELL YOURSELF: "Take me instead—or, better yet,
take a stranger!"

You can't bring back your loved one, but you can fill the void
left behind by trying to bargain with your local electronics
store for an equally fulfilling relationship with an LCD TV.

STAGE 4.
DEPRESSION

TELL YOURSELF: "Sure, I'm staying in bed all day,
but look at all the sadness I'm sweating out."

Focus on your positive memories to get over the depression
of mourning. Then slide back into the everyday depression
of living in a world where death is even possible.

STAGE 5.
ACCEPTANCE

TELL YOURSELF: "I don't even remember the dead person."

Take comfort in the fact that if you can't bring people back to
life, you can at least outlive them.

A NATURAL PROCESS
Death is just a part of life. Specifically,
the last, worst part.

Moving

Whether you're relocating for a new job or skipping town because the current mayor isn't you, there's one world-class metropolis that welcomes winners with open arms: Flagstaff, Arizona!

▶ Leave your neighbors in the dust, literally, by demolishing your current home.

▶ Don't bother packing any items that are heavy or crying. Instead, furnish your new home with housewares from Flagstaff's many artisanal craftspeople.

▶ Buy the biggest house available to hold all your new memories. Your oversized abode will signal to the local Flagstaffers that you are definitely best friend material.

▶ Do you like craters? Flagstaff is home to both the historic Meteor Crater and Sunset Crater Volcano National Monument. The only thing that won't crater is your excitement!

▶ Host a housewarming party and invite Flagstaff native son Ted Danson. Get his address from the Flagstaff Tourism Board— the only tourism board forward-thinking enough to sponsor individual chapters of books. See you soon, neighbor!

WHY MOVE ANYWHERE ELSE?

VENICE: In tranquil Flagstaff, your kids can play ball in the street. Try doing that in Venice—*they'll drown.*

CHICAGO: When Al Capone's ghost comes back, what city do you think he'll be terrorizing first?

YUMA, ARIZONA: If you want to move to a place named after the sound of someone throwing up, be our guest.

WHY DO THEY CALL IT "FLAGSTAFF?"
We could tell you, but you're better off moving there and finding out!

Nailing a Job Interview

Other than panning for gemstones and computer-aided wishing, getting a job is the surest way to secure an income—but you'll have to impress the stuffed shirt from HR first. Dazzle job interviewers with these tenacious techniques:

OFFER A STRONG HANDSHAKE

Your open palm will indicate that you're not concealing any weapons, while your forceful grip will demonstrate that you don't *need* any.

MAINTAIN EYE CONTACT

Very smart people do not need to blink.

STAY ON YOUR TOES

During a job interview, your interlocutor will attempt to sabotage your prospects with dozens of "gotcha" questions like, "Would you like a glass of water?" and "Nice meeting you." The answer to both questions is *no*.

PROJECT CONFIDENCE

If they ask you where you see yourself in five years, reply, "Exactly two years older."

BE FLEXIBLE

During the final stage of the interview, you will be asked to murder your predecessor. Say "No" to earn the interviewer's respect or say "Yes" to earn a job.

Weaknesses are for the Weak

■ ■ ■

When a job interviewer asks, "What is your greatest weakness?" reply, "I work so hard that I often forget to pay attention or complete assignments."

THE PERFECT RÉSUMÉ

Stand out from the stack by writing your résumé on high-quality paper stock, such as a repurposed wedding invitation or a hundred-dollar bill, or in very fine print at the bottom of a more accomplished person's résumé.

DRESS FOR SUCCESS

Wisdom dictates that one should "Dress for the job you want, not the job you have," which is why most job interviewees sport a dolphin trainer's wetsuit, professor's beret, and ceremonial rapier. Serious job seekers need each of these items in their wardrobe:

POWER TIE

Usually a snake worn around the neck to bite rivals.

BLAZER

Should have the nickname "Blazer" written across the shoulders in flaming letters.

BLUE JEANS

To be burned during your
job interview as you shout,
"I'll never wear *these* again!"

MAGIC RING OF INVISIBILITY

Keep it secret; keep it safe.

A SMILE

People will never know
that you're really thinking,
"I would eat everyone
here."

Nurturing Houseplants

Indoor gardeners of all skill levels know that, like money, plants don't just grow on trees, they need to be nurtured. Beat Mother Nature at her own game by growing plants where they don't belong—indoors:

OBEY THEIR THIRST Make sure to water your plants 24/7— that's twenty-four times a year for seven hours straight. The exceptions are cacti, which synthesize their own water from the blood of people who accidentally touch them.

LET THE SUN SHINE Plants require plenty of sunlight, unlike humans, who need only the light of their television or computer to remain happy.

EDUCATE = CULTIVATE Read to your floral wards. They can't hear you, but it's a good excuse to read more.

PUMP UP THE VOLUME Barrage your plants with music. The sound vibrations will stimulate them enough to make them want to have sex with other plants and reproduce.

MUNCH ON MULCH You can make your own compost from the decomposing bodies of other houseplants you took such good care of that they died of happiness.

FLORA OR FAUNA?

Be careful before committing to a houseplant—
it might technically be an animal. Here's a look at
commonly misidentified flora and fauna:

VENUS FLYTRAP

FLORA OR FAUNA? FLORA.

Despite its craving for flesh, the Venus flytrap is technically a
plant because it receives its nutrients through photosynthesis
and only kills for fun.

CORAL

FLORA OR FAUNA? FLORA.

Something that looks this much like a plant must be a plant.

THE GREEN-BELLIED TREE FROG

FLORA OR FAUNA? NEITHER.

The green-bellied tree frog is neither a tree nor a frog because it
went extinct in 1992.

QUICKSAND

FLORA OR FAUNA? FAUNA.

It may not be the smartest animal in the zoo, but once it has
you in its grasp, the only way to escape is to swim down to the
bottom and punch it in the nose.

Optical Illusions

Scientists and hucksters often use deceptive visual illusions to confuse your consciousness, leaving you vulnerable to self-reflection and its crippling corollary, doubt. For the first time ever, here are the answers to these puzzles of perception:

fig. 1

DO YOU SEE A RABBIT OR A DUCK?

ANSWER: This is neither a rabbit nor a duck. It's clearly a river otter with a clothespin jammed into its brain.

BEAUTIFUL SYMMETRY

Psychologists will tell you there's no correct answer for a Rorschach inkblot test, but they'll be secretly disappointed if you don't answer, "Sex perverts doing pervert stuff."

fig. 2

DO YOU SEE AN OLD LADY OR A BEAUTIFUL YOUNG WOMAN?

ANSWER: Women of any age are beautiful!

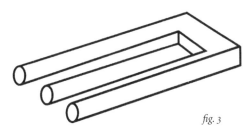

fig. 3

**WHAT'S THE DEAL WITH THIS THING?
HOW CAN THE . . . GO INTO THE . . . ? OH, MAN.**

ANSWER: It's simple: The middle rod is totally disconnected from everything, just like a recent divorcé who doesn't even care that the dog was licking his slice of pizza while he was in the bathroom for an hour.

fig. 4

WHICH OF THESE MEN IS BIGGER?

ANSWER: Looks, like lies, can be deceiving. Both men are the same size.

fig. 5

IS THIS A PICTURE OF A VASE OR OF TWO FACES?

ANSWER: It's the faces of those same two guys from the previous optical illusion. Is there anything they *can't* do?

THE MAZE of LIFE

Now that your eyes have been trained to overcome every illusion, you should be able to effortlessly navigate this metaphorical maze instantaneously:

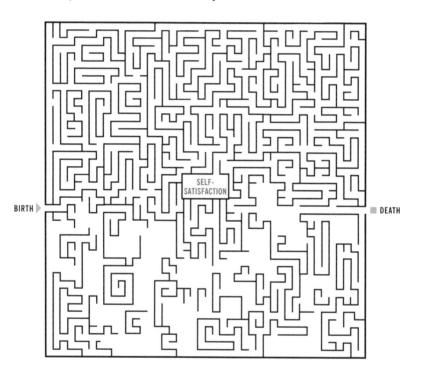

BIRTH ▶   ■ DEATH

SELF-SATISFACTION

TROPICAL ILLUSION

Every year, 40,000 Americans are killed by mirages.

Poker

Proficient poker players know when to hold 'em, know when to fold 'em, and know when they're ensnared in a cycle of victory and loss so irresistibly euphoric that they can't stop even when they're ahead. Study the hierarchy of these winning poker hands to raise the stakes and your game:

10. HIGH CARD If the players' hands do not contain at least one pair, the winner is determined by whoever can throw his card the highest.

9. A PAIR Two cards of the same rank, suit, or approximate size and shape.

8. TWO PAIR Also known as a pair of twos—the most valuable pair in the game, as there are only two twos in the entire deck.

7. THREE PAIR It's difficult to get three pairs in a five-card hand . . . but not impossible.

6. STRAIGHT No matter how poor your hand is, if you can be straight with the other players and admit it, you'll win.

5. DEALER'S DODGE Replace one of your cards with a hundred dollar bill to immediately boost your hand's value by a hundred dollars.

4. FULL HOUSE Any hand that has been used to construct a house of cards sturdy enough to withstand ten nail-biting seconds of all the other players blowing on it.

3. JACK-IN-THE-HOLE Any combination of face cards that allow you to spell "A JAQK?"

2. ROYAL FLUSH If you're skilled enough to be dealt this hand containing the entire royal family, let their unsmiling visages fill the hole left by your real family.

1. THE DEAD MAN'S HAND Two black aces and two black eights. This hand was famously held by Wild Bill Hickok, President McKinley, and all the passengers on the *Titanic*.

IDENTIFYING TELLS

All players have subconscious "tells" that give away when they're lying. Become unbluffable by watching out for these common tells:

- ♥ Visible perspiration
- ♣ Darting eyes
- ♦ Involuntary trickle of ear blood
- ♠ "Truthman's Grin"
- ♥ Suspiciously unrelated boasting ("WOW! What a tremendous hand—hand, of course, referring to the unit of measurement for describing a horse's height, equal to increments of four inches or 10.16 centimeters.")

- ♠ Yellow steam shooting out of nostrils
- ♥ Cussin'
- ♦ Hair getting noticeably longer
- ♣ Accidentally holding cards facing outward
- ♠ Crying

Potlucks

There's no luck involved in bringing the most popular dish to the casual, yet high-stakes community gathering that is the traditional potluck. Shame your culinary competitors/neighbors by bringing the most tasted and talked-about dish:

KNOW YOUR AUDIENCE

Scour the list of invitees to determine if your shared fare should be geared toward pizza-loving teens, gluten-free diabetics, or vegetarians who make exceptions for meat that smells good.

PERFORM RECONNAISSANCE

Is Shirley making her famous Vodka-Soaked Gummi Bear Casserole? Is Hector getting his priest cousin to sprinkle holy water on a turducken? Stage a phony potluck the day before to trick neighbors into revealing their dishes prematurely.

WORK UNDER THE COVER OF DARKNESS

Stay up all night making practice meals then give them to the less fortunate, such as neighborhood raccoons.

MAKE EXTRA

That way, you have enough to literally rub it in your neighbors' faces.

ENJOY THE TASTE OF VICTORY

Devour a disproportionate, stomach-straining amount of your neighbors' dishes, ensuring that fellow guests will be forced to eat the food you brought or go hungry.

Winning a Pie-Eating Contest

Summertime potlucks often culminate in an old-fashioned pie-eating contest. Each type of pie requires a different approach:

APPLE PIE: Eat as many pies as you can in the allotted time!

BLUEBERRY PIE: Consume more pies than your competitors before the clock runs out!

BANANA CREAM PIE: Even when you feel impossibly full, keep eating!

PECAN PIE: Eat slowly and steadily or, better yet, eat as quickly as possible the entire time!

STRAWBERRY-RHUBARB PIE: Eat the most pies!

Puberty

ATTENTION, READER: You are permitted to read only your gender-appropriate chapter on conquering puberty. Learning about the opposite sex is considered too arousing.

PUBERTY FOR BOYS

Harness your raging torrents of teenage hormones and confusion to win at puberty. Listen to your body to ensure stronger muscles, thicker chest hair, and more vivid nocturnal emissions than your peers:

① FACIAL FOLLICLES: Thicken your peach fuzz into a sexy scruff by holding your breath for two hours a day to force more hair out of your face.

② HAIR IN UNEXPECTED PLACES: Bonus body hair is a locker-room status symbol, especially when shaved into the shape of a downward-pointing arrow or naked lady.

③ ENGORGED NAVEL: It'll keep visibly swelling and swelling until you lose your virginity. Hurry!

④ THE MALE BONER: Your penis will become erect when aroused, grazed by a slight breeze, or that one time when you accidentally saw your sister naked in the shower and you just happened to have an erection at the time and it screwed you both up for life.

⑤ DESCENDED GONADS: Don't be alarmed when your baby testicles fall out to make room for your permanent testicles.

⑥ ACNE: Acquire as much as possible–today's debilitating blemishes are tomorrow's roguish scars.

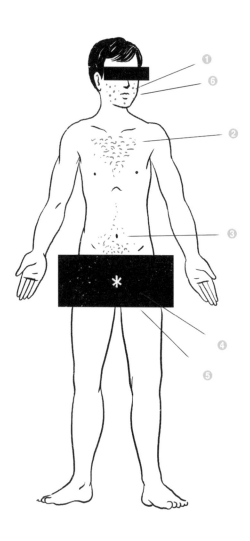

ATTENTION, READER: Disregard the prior instruction. Women are also permitted to read the male's section, but not vice-versa. Boys are not mature enough to handle it.

PUBERTY FOR GIRLS

The harrowing transition from spritely, innocent girl to stately, mystique-belching woman is best completed as quickly as possible. Luckily, modern superhormones in store-bought milk can usher you into the grown-up world of glamour and vaginal bleeding faster than ever:

1 **INCREASED HEIGHT:** You'll experience a growth spurt before your male counterparts, giving you the evolutionary advantage of surviving longer in quicksand.

2 **BREASTS:** Ideally you'll develop at least two.

3 **BROADER HIPS:** Although evolved to carry infants during pregnancy, your new, stronger hips are best used to kick over tractors and house the second set of kidneys you'll grow during puberty.

4 **PUBIC HAIR:** Should naturally form into a neatly trimmed triangle or grow in completely shaved.

5 **VAGINA:** When fully developed, will look exactly like a Georgia O'Keeffe painting.

6 **FINE, SEXY ANKLES:** When you reach adulthood, it's time to finally show off the naughty gliding joints between the distal ends of the tibia and fibula that drive men wild.

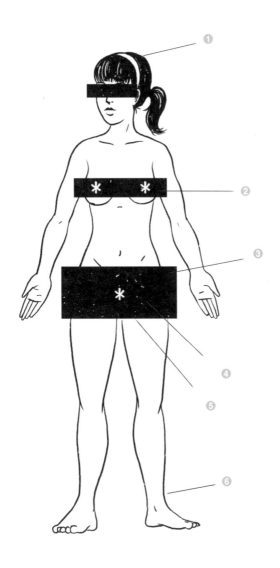

YOUR CHANGING VOICE

Your once-squeaky soprano will deepen into a manly baritone immediately after fulfilling the teenage social requirement of trying cigarettes. Expect your voice to go through the following phases before arriving at the ability to impersonate your dad on the phone:

1. cracking

2. volume unpredictability

3. megavoice

4. donald duck–mouth

5. ultra–high-frequency pitch audible only to dogs and girls who think of you as just a friend

YOUR FIRST CRUSH

As you begin puberty, you will inevitably become infatuated with your era's most swoonable teen idol. Before devoting yourself, make sure the object of your puppy love meets all of the following teen idol requirements:

1. pillow lips

2. the haircut of a girl

3. publicly demonstrated support for animal-based charity and/or has diabetes

4. nonthreatening foray into hip-hop

5. all of the songs seem to be about . . . you?!

Public Speaking

All of history's greatest and/or most evil leaders have excelled at enthralling audiences with their words. Even if you have a phobia of public speaking, you can project utter confidence and sway any audience with this crowd-captivating routine:

STEP 1. OPEN WITH A JOKE: "A funny thing happened to me on the way over here. I was trying to determine the deal with airplane food . . . *and I wasn't able to!*" [Pause for laughter]

STEP 2. MAKE EYE CONTACT: Using your fingertips, make contact with as many of the audience members' eyeballs as possible.

STEP 3. DELIVER A PRECISE, WELL-REASONED ARGUMENT: Or, better yet, karate chop through a brick wall with the word *TAXES* spray-painted on it.

STEP 4. DISPARAGE DISSENTERS: "Now, some folks may disagree with me, but to them I respectfully say, maybe you'd see things my way if you weren't so busy eating poop on Planet Butthead."

STEP 5. FINISH STRONG: Rouse your crowd by leading them in a hip-hop version of the national anthem, releasing a flock of inspiring swans, and bringing out a cadre of religious leaders to legally marry you to everyone in the audience.

GET A STANDING O

YOU CAN COMPEL ANY AUDIENCE
TO RISE TO ITS FEET BY:

- Shouting, "Stand up if you if you love freedom and hate bad diseases!"

- Dangling a fishing line strung with cash just out of the crowd's reach.

- Setting off the fire alarm.

PICTURE THE AUDIENCE NAKED

Since you're standing behind a podium, no one will notice your now-raging erection.

Quitting Smoking

Giving up cigarettes is one of the toughest things a person can do. Show your brain and body who's boss by overcoming this chemical dependency, so you can live free of addiction and start smoking again—on your *own* terms:

STEP 1 ▶ **Gradually dial down your dosage.** Cut your cigarettes in half lengthwise. This will give you half the tobacco you're used to and give you the chance to smoke twice as many.

STEP 2 ▶ **Break bad habits.** If you're used to having a smoke after taking a shower or eating a meal, stop doing these things immediately.

STEP 3 ▶ **Keep your hands busy.** Learn some impressive magic tricks that will prove as welcome in social situations as second-hand smoke.

STEP 4 ▶ **Satisfy your oral fixation.** Do this by shouting all the time.

THE JURY IS STILL OUT

Scientists still disagree about whether cigarettes are truly addictive or if they're just so deliciously satisfying that folks can't stop smoking them.

STEP 5 ▶ **Curb your craving.** Wear a nicotine patch and gnaw on a hunk of nicotine gum (a.k.a., chewing tobacco).

STEP 6 ▶ **Admit your addiction.** Before you can start the process of quitting, you must first admit that you have a problem. If for some reason you didn't complete Step 6 first, you must start over from the beginning.

STEP 7 ▶ **Create a Pavlovian aversion to smoking.** Drink a glass of disgusting gin every time you crave a cigarette.

STEP 8 ▶ **Commemorate your triumph over addiction to smoking with a celebratory Cuban cigar.**

Raising a Child or Small Dog

When raising your smallest and most dependent family member, you must prepare them to reach their highest possible peak of success, (slightly lower than your own level of success). Give your baby or baby dog every advantage by performing these nurturing tasks:

Feed them daily ☑ DOG ☑ BABY

Foster an emotional connection by rubbing their belly ☑ DOG ☑ BABY

Shout their name at them until they begin responding to it ☑ DOG ☑ BABY

As they begin to move around on all fours, cordon off concrete basement stairs with those wooden gates ☑ DOG ☑ BABY

Have them checked out by a veterinarian ☑ DOG ☑ BABY

Naming Rights

Your baby or dog will respond most readily to a monosyllabic name ending in a hard consonant such as *Max*, *Blog*, or *Cat*.

Raising a Child or Small Dog

Teach them a lesson by rubbing their nose in their mistakes	☑ DOG *(literally)* ☑ BABY *(metaphorically)*
Start saving money to give them a first-rate education	☑ DOG ☐ BABY
Take them to an R-rated movie	☐ DOG ☑ BABY
Account for their sudden disappearance by explaining that you "sent them to a farm in the country"	☑ DOG ☐ BABY *(worth thinking about?)*

EARLY EDUCATION

Set your baby or puppy up for overachievement with these equally applicable developmental enhancers:

→ Sit them in front of a TV and have them watch hours of *Baby Einstein, Baby Mozart, Baby Chomsky, Baby Darwin,* or *Baby Jesus.*

→ Keep your infant or canine in peak physical condition by tying them to a leash and having them run on all fours alongside your bicycle.

→ Use your hands to physically mold their mouths and tongues into the shapes necessary for human speech.

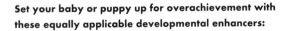

Some ambitious households contain puppies and babies.
The ideal time to introduce them is in the womb,
by rubbing the mother's bulging tummy with a pregnant dog.

Reading

Reading is the ultimate combination of boring and time-consuming, but you can quickly synthesize the sum of recorded human knowledge by reading for speed, comprehension, and theme:

READING FOR SPEED

By reading only the first and last word of every sentence, you can glean the author's intent without wasting time on the flowery prose. Test your ability below:

> By age seven, all children should understand the importance of reading. This fundamental skill is critical no matter what skeptics tell you. Have the sense to instill its value into your children forever. Pledged to education, they'll learn concepts like the difference between "you're" and "your." Soul, mind, and body benefit from teachers being listened to. The literate mind is the one most prepared to evade the grasp of the devil.

READING FOR COMPREHENSION

Read the following paragraph as quickly as possible and then answer the comprehension questions below to test your ability to retain key details:

> Joe the bus driver sat behind the steering wheel, wearing his blue hat. The clock read 8:59. He stopped at the intersection of Birch and 15th Street. A young woman, Maureen, boarded the bus, carrying seven plastic grocery bags. It began to rain.

COMPREHENSION QUESTIONS:

1. What is the bus driver's name?

2. Did Maureen know the bus driver's name?

3. Was she carrying enough groceries to feed a boyfriend?

4. What would Joe have said if he'd had the courage to talk to Maureen?

5. When did it start raining?

ANSWERS:

5. Never: It was just the tears in Joe's eyes.

4. "So . . . do you like buses—No! That sounds so STUPID!"

3. Joe wondered the same thing.

2. Of course not.

1. Joe

Relating to Your Grandkids

Readers of normal age are encouraged to cut out this chapter and present it to their grandparents to help them talk to other generations.

Today's youngsters may have soda pop where their manners should be, but cultivating a relationship with them can gain you a hungry ear for your war stories, and a calming presence when you find out the president is black. Hold your grandchildren's interest by subtly making your stories more relatable to young people:

- Refer to your **HARDSCRABBLE CHILDHOOD** as "an era when kids legally could, and had to, smoke cigarettes."

- Call out **THE GREAT DEPRESSION** for what it really was—a rad time when dust was plentiful and nobody had to work.

- **CRISP, REFRESHING COCA-COLA** is still crisp, refreshing Coca-Cola but now it's thirty times more expensive, and we know that's it's basically poison.

- Describe **HITLER** as "a freakish mix of Darth Vader and the lawyers who sue people for downloading MP3s."

GET MORE VISITS

KIDS LOVE CANDY, SO MAKE SURE YOUR SOAPS LOOK AS MUCH LIKE CANDY AS POSSIBLE.

- Replace **INSPIRING STORY ABOUT RISING FROM POVERTY, PUTTING YOURSELF THROUGH SCHOOL**, and **WORKING IN A MILL FOR FIFTY YEARS** with "hustlin'."

- Instead of **SYPHILIS**, mention nothing to your grandchildren about contracting syphilis.

THE PERFECT BIRTHDAY GIFT

To determine how much cash to slip into your grandkids' birthday cards, use the following equation: Their current age, multiplied by the number of times they've called you in the past year, plus five dollars.

Representing Yourself In Court

Your judicial right of *pro se* allows you to represent yourself in court, even without any legal training. Get off scot-free by filling in the blanks below. Your opening argument will be so airtight you won't need a closing argument:

Thank you, (YOUR HONOR / LADIES AND GENTLEMEN OF THE JURY / F.O.R.E.M.A.N. 9000 GUILT-DETERMINATION APP).

I stand before you a humble (GENDER), (OCCUPATION), and (ADJECTIVE) citizen of this (CITY / COUNTY / GODLESS LIBERTARIAN SEASTEAD).

For that reason, I am entering the plea of (NOT GUILTY / INSANITY / TOO BENEFICIAL TO SOCIETY TO INCARCERATE).

You see, on (DATE OF ALLEGED OFFENSE), I was falsely accused of the heinous crime of (UNLICENSED ARSON / PARKING MY CAR ON A FOOTBALL FIELD / OTHER APPLICABLE CHARGES). However, I will present (STARTLING EVIDENCE / DOZENS OF SURPRISE WITNESSES / HIGHLY PLAUSIBLE FABRICATIONS) that prove(s) my (INNOCENCE / MAGNIFICENCE) in this matter.

First, we must ask the question: (WHAT IS GUILT?/ ISN'T SOCIETY TO BLAME? / LOOK OUT, A SKUNK GOT INTO THE COURTROOM!) To this, I say: I take (FULL / PARTIAL / JUST ENOUGH) responsibility for my (ACTIONS / INACTIONS / COURT SKUNKS).

However, I have a foolproof alibi: On the (DATE OF OFFENSE), I was (WORKING LATE / DONATING NOT INCONSIDERABLE SUMS TO CHARITY / BUSY NOT COMMITTING CRIMES). Also, I am on record as a notable supporter of (ANIMALS / IMPOVERISHED CHILDREN / INVITING JURY MEMBERS TO MY HOUSE FOR A POOL PARTY).

Although the facts of the case are against me, it will shock you to learn that the real criminal is (SITTING IN THIS COURTROOM RIGHT NOW / SITTING IN THE WHITE HOUSE RIGHT NOW / MY DIABOLICAL TWIN COUSIN)!

In conclusion, wasn't it Thurgood Marshall who said, '(VERB) (ADVERB) (SUBJECT) skunks under your chairs?' Go, (NAME OF LOCAL FOOTBALL FRANCHISE)!"

LEGAL LOOPHOLE

If you're able to grab the judge's gavel, you can dismiss your case by declaring "Freedom!" and banging it against the bailiff's Bible.

SELECTING YOUR JURY

Be sure to have each of the following archetypes on your jury to ensure your acquittal:

THE SCHOOLTEACHER

Can educate other jurors on the difference between right and wrong, and is easily bribed with apples.

THE BLUE-COLLAR DAD

Will always side with the underdog, so make yourself look extra-guilty.

THE PREACHER

Thinks only God can judge people, so is contractually obligated to vote "not guilty."

THE WELL-KNOWN CELEBRITY IN OLD MAN MAKEUP

Though doing his best to serve his civic duty anonymously, his star power can't help but illuminate your case.

YOU OBJECT!

STEER COURTROOM PROCEEDINGS IN YOUR FAVOR BY SHOUTING THESE TIMELY INTERJECTIONS:

▶ "Objection—leading the witness!"

▶ "Objection—too sexy!"

▶ "Objection—incredibly damning!"

THE BITTER FORMER DISTRICT ATTORNEY

Is sure to vote "not guilty" just to stick it to his successor.

THE DEATH PENALTY OPPONENT

Will guarantee that you're not hanged. Hung? Hanged? Hanged.

THE BABY

Their metaphorical innocence will rub off on you.

YOUR FORMER SPOUSE

You've had your ups and downs, but your ex will remember the good times.

HENRY FONDA

He *always* votes "not guilty"!

THE COMPUTER HACKER

Can hack into the court's data banks to change your verdict from "guilty" to "maximum rad!"

GARBAGE BAG FULL OF DOVES

Granted suffrage by the Nineteenth Amendment, the doves will burst forth triumphantly when you're pronounced innocent.

YOURSELF

It'd be tempting to just vote "not guilty," but you have a responsibility to weigh the evidence.

Running a Marathon

Most people consider completing a marathon to be a victory in itself, but these long-distance liars are running from the truth: in all sports, *one* individual is always the winner. Finish first and endure the physical, mental, and literal hurdles your body will experience during this 26.2-mile gauntlet of endurance:

MILE 1

Pace yourself by setting the fastest possible pace for yourself. Immediately sprint out of the runner's corral and never drop below top speed.

TRAINER'S TIP: Warm up your muscles before the race by inhaling a bunch of hot cigarette smoke. ☆

MILE 5

You'll begin to emit a thin layer of perspiration. Ignore it— it's just your body's way of signaling that it's not sure why you're trying to kill it.

TRAINER'S TIP: Stay hydrated and carbohydrated by grabbing an en route cup of water and a bank logo–emblazoned sports bottle full of travel spaghetti. ☆

MILE 9

Halfway there . . . *psych*! But tell yourself that to prevent
your Achilles tendon from spontaneously petrifying out of
hopelessness.

> **TRAINER'S TIP:** Remember the words of your beloved
> high school track coach, "I never touched you! Tell them I never
> touched you!" ☆

MILE 20

To trigger a second wind, your body will jettison any extraneous
bones that might be slowing you down.

> **TRAINER'S TIP:** Embrace the runner's high—a hallucinato-
> ry dreamscape in which a swarm of cooing bats gently carries you
> toward the finish line. Not to be confused with a real swarm of
> motivational bats that will be released at mile marker 24. ☆

MILE 26

During the last 0.2 miles, unleash your body's final momentum
reserve by repeatedly punching one of your kidneys until it
dissolves into a cocktail of pure liquid energy.

> **TRAINER'S TIP:** As you cross the finish line, outshine the
> marathon's inventor, Pheidippides, by not dying immediately
> afterward. ☆

RUNNING FOR CHARITY

Real winners help out losers by running in marathons for prominent charities like:

▸ **THE BREAST CANCER FOUNDATION**

▸ **THE *BEST* CANCER FOUNDATION** (A COMPETING BREAST CANCER CHARITY)

▸ **SAVE THE SOCIETY TO SAVE THE WHALES**

▸ **THE BORING CHILDREN'S FUND**

▸ **THE POSSIBLY INNOCENT MURDERERS PROJECT**

Shopping

Expert shoppers are able to hunt down the best bargains so they can avoid tarnishing their carts with cheap goods. Steer clear of last season's pieces of garbage and win at shopping by bringing home the real bargain—something expensive:

MAKE A SHOPPING LIST Then throw it away. You shouldn't be bound by anyone's constraints—even your own.

SELECT YOUR CART Climb into the provided children's seat and demand to be ferried around by a stout employee. This will keep your hands free for grabbing items more quickly.

OUTMUSCLE OTHER CUSTOMERS Why engage in a tug-of-war for that last must-have Christmas gift? Instead, make a heartfelt handmade version, then use it to deceive the other shoppers so you can grab the superior store-bought model.

HAGGLE AS NECESSARY Don't accept the price as marked—demand to pay even more to show the shopkeeper who they're dealing with.

CONSUME CONSPICUOUSLY Don't limit yourself to shopping only for items that are for sale. For instance, does anyone own the Eiffel Tower, or the Internet? Everything has a price.

RETURNING MERCHANDISE

**If you need to return a recent purchase, use the provided
item-specific justifications for a hassle-free refund:**

ALARM CLOCK	"Makes an annoying ringing sound at least once per day."
MICROWAVE	"Placing the microwave in the oven did not cause food to cook four times as fast."
PANTS	"Fit well, looked good, but left torso completely unprotected."
PC	"Internet pornography not as interesting or alarming as I'd hoped."
SPOOKY OLD MANSION	"Haunted."
CAR	"Accidentally bought for beautiful daughter's fifteenth birthday."
DOG	"Died immediately several months after purchase."
SNOW GLOBE	"Kept waking up trapped inside" or "Never woke up trapped inside even once."
JAWS ON VHS	"I don't own a damn VCR!"
ENCYCLOPEDIA	"Contains no information whatsoever on why my girlfriend is mad at me."
THIS BOOK	See opposite page.

NOW IF CLERK DECLARES TO YOU WITH ARMS FOLDED
"BOOK THAT SHOWS DAMAGE OR CREASED PAGES CAN'T BE RETURNED"
THANKS TO YOUR SMILE, HE'LL MAKE EXCEPTION FOR
YOUR OTHERWISE COMPLETELY NON-REFUNDABLE PURCHASE

Stock Market

Playing the stock market is no get-rich-quick scheme, but it *is* a foolproof wealth-generating strategy that will help you get rich—and quick! Turn a volatile maelstrom of trillions of unpredictable factors into free money by buying, selling, or holding according to these stock-affecting scenarios:

▶ **Little-known tech startup invents an algorithm that lets users smell new babies over the Internet:** BUY

▶ **Auto manufacturer forced to recall car that blows up when the driver is sad:** SELL

▶ **Struggling financial firm introduces new Chief Financial Officer that's just a big bag of money wearing expensive-looking glasses:** HOLD

▶ **Soft-drink company releases groundbreaking advertisement featuring hip, diverse twentysomethings enjoying themselves:** BUY

▶ **Big box retailer's company headquarters rises from its foundation and sprouts mechanical crab legs:** BUY

WHAT IS A BLUE CHIP COMPANY?
It's a company that makes those blue tortilla chips they have at fancy markets.

▶ CFO Bag of Money Wearing Glasses found dead in Dubai hotel room of a self-inflicted gunshot wound: SELL

▶ Oil company executives circulate desperate, hand-drawn map revealing "hidden cache of oil . . . in the moon?": SELL

▶ Fast food conglomerate cuts costs by replacing genuine sour cream with nothing: HOLD

▶ Pharmaceutical company invents sexually transmitted cancer just to see if they could: SELL

▶ CFO Bag of Money's steadfast son installed as new CFO, vowing "to be an Even Bigger Bag of Money, with even more money in it.": BUY

ADVANCED INVESTMENT PRINCIPLES 101

BUY LOW, SELL HIGH, BUY HIGH

Start out by buying a near-worthless stock that other investors have given up on. Patiently wait until it skyrockets in value and then sell it off, using the profits to buy back the stock now that it's way more valuable.

RAKE IT IN

Enjoy the perks of a true Wall Street tycoon by literally raking your money into large piles and hiring a team of plucky orphans to weep as you burn it in front of them.

TRACK MARKET CHANGES

Consult this graph of historical and forecast market performance to find the ideal time to invest:

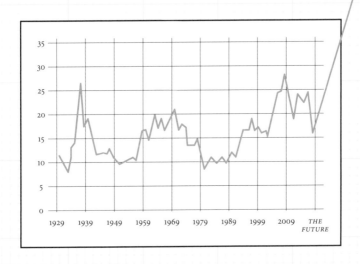

Surviving a Breakup

As you reach stratospheric levels of success, your current romantic partner will inevitably be seized by uncontrollable feelings of jealousy. Win your soon-to-be-terminated romance by making a clean break and handling your jilting with conspicuous confidence:

💜 **Don't set your former flame's clothes on fire.** Pack them neatly into a box visibly labeled "Discarded Medical Penises" and dare them to carry it home.

💜 **Get into a rebound relationship.** Sleep with your ex's ugliest boss, an astronaut they admired as a child, or a parade of strangers with their same first and last name.

💜 **Don't childishly take their number out of your phone.** Instead, smash the phone in front them and shout, "This is how much I love you!"

💜 **Get into shape.** Remember, a blubbering ball of uncontrollable sobbing is technically a shape.

💜 **Prove how over them you are.** Jokingly ask them to marry you. If they say, "Yes," sarcastically settle down with them, start a family, and live out the rest of your days in marital bliss.

THE BEST PART OF BREAKING UP

After a breakup, you can look forward to some hot makeup sex—the sex you'll have to make up in your imagination because you just lost the last person who will ever find you attractive.

BREAKDOWN of
POST-BREAKUP THOUGHTS

AFTER A BREAKUP, HERE'S HOW YOU'LL ALLOCATE
YOUR MENTAL ENERGY:

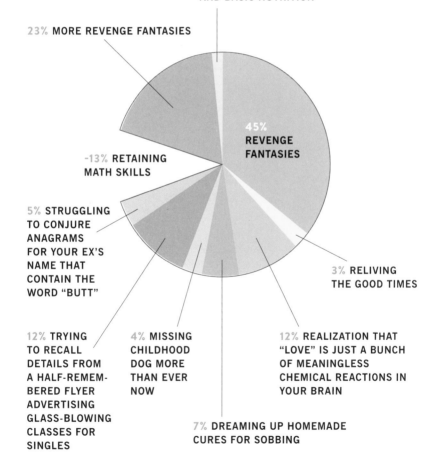

2% WORK, PERSONAL GROOMING, AND BASIC NUTRITION

23% MORE REVENGE FANTASIES

45% REVENGE FANTASIES

-13% RETAINING MATH SKILLS

5% STRUGGLING TO CONJURE ANAGRAMS FOR YOUR EX'S NAME THAT CONTAIN THE WORD "BUTT"

3% RELIVING THE GOOD TIMES

12% TRYING TO RECALL DETAILS FROM A HALF-REMEM-BERED FLYER ADVERTISING GLASS-BLOWING CLASSES FOR SINGLES

4% MISSING CHILDHOOD DOG MORE THAN EVER NOW

12% REALIZATION THAT "LOVE" IS JUST A BUNCH OF MEANINGLESS CHEMICAL REACTIONS IN YOUR BRAIN

7% DREAMING UP HOMEMADE CURES FOR SOBBING

Talking on the Phone with Your Mom

A phone call from your mother can be a garden of encouragement or a minefield of judgment. When confronted with these eight topics that your mother will inevitably raise during every phone call, reply with these psychologically precise, mother-mollifying responses:

YOUR CAREER PROGRESS	"I'm advancing at a rate comparable to my peers! My college degree is really coming in handy despite the perceived lack of real-world applications of my major!"
YOUR RELATIONSHIP STATUS	"The previous relationship advice you gave me was correct! I am closer to marriage than before!"
YOUR REACTION TO A RECENT CARE PACKAGE	"Thanks! Even though I am a grown-up, all this stuff from my childhood bedroom has found a welcome place in my adult home. And the local newspaper articles you sent were incredibly enlightening!"

NEWS ABOUT BARELY REMEMBERED RELATIVES	"I am happy/sad to hear that. I care about them as much as you do."
INQUIRIES ABOUT YOUR FRIENDS WHO SHE LIKES BETTER THAN YOU	"My college roommate is having equivalent success. We are still just as close as you imagine."
LONG SYNOPSIS OF THE CURRENT SEASON OF *BURN NOTICE*	"Uh-huh."
DAD SHOUTING FROM THE OTHER ROOM	"Tell Dad I gave him due credit for his recent barbecue secret but did not reveal it."
INCREASINGLY CONSERVATIVE POLITICAL DIATRIBE	"More people of my generation should agree with you. I have to go right now."

BEWARE MOTHERLY ADVICE

Mothers are inherently untrustworthy due to their baffling tendency to offer unconditional love and support to even society's most useless members: babies.

Tactful Excuses to Hang Up on Your Mother

When a phone call with your mother has run its course but she hasn't realized it yet, deploy one of these careful conversation enders:

▶ "Oh! My oven timer appears to be going off, from one of those recipes you handed down to me."

▶ "Gotta go compile a list of possible grandchild names."

▶ "I must finally admit it—you've had the wrong number all these years. I am just a friendly, unrelated person who has enjoyed talking to you."

▶ (Put the phone down without hanging up and pick it back up at any time later. She'll still be having the conversation.)

TALKING ON THE PHONE WITH YOUR MOM

Volunteering and Not Even Making a Big Deal About It

The highest form of charity is to help the less fortunate anonymously, thus unfairly depriving you of the recognition you so righteously deserve. Here's how to get credit for serving your community without looking like you want credit for serving your community:

VOLUNTEER AT A SOUP KITCHEN Refuse a name tag and instead pour a handful of business cards into every bowl of soup that you serve.

READ TO THE BLIND but give every book a thrilling bonus chapter about a noble stranger who reads to the blind and also stops an experimental bullet train from going kablooey.

DONATE FUNDS TO BUILD A NEW MATERNITY WARD Decline to have the building named after you in exchange for having all the babies named after you.

CHARITY BEGINS AT HOME

You don't have to get off the couch to become the savior of your community:

. . . .

- Start an organic mushroom garden in your bathroom tiles.

- Teach your kids a second language like Spanish or hiding their feelings.

- Give 10 percent of your income to scientists working on a cure for poverty.

WORK TO IMPROVE OPEN SPACE Help the Parks Department overcome its lack of inspirational statuary by modeling for a statue of Aidos, the Greek goddess of humility.

LEAVE A LASTING PHILANTHROPIC LEGACY Adopt every homeless animal in your community, then coat them in double-sided tape to pick up litter along the highway.

DO IT FOR THE KIDS

Teach the youth of your community self-reliance by becoming a youth mentor and then never showing up.

NOBLE CAUSES

You can make an impact by devoting all of your charitable energy to one of these worthy causes:

Saving the rec center

Rescuing the community center

Raising money to save the youth center

Preserving the after-school hangout spot for teens

Saving local businesses by turning the rec center into a desperately needed parking lot

TEACH A MAN TO FISH

Give a man a fish, and he'll eat for a day. Teach a man to fish, and he'll compete with you for all the fish in the lake. He must be stopped.

Wilderness Survival Using Only this Book

You must also assert your superiority over nature. Willfully strand yourself in the wild to prove that you can conquer the elements by turning this book itself into the survival staples you'll need:

fig. 1

CANTEEN

Hollow out the pages of the book and line the compartment with banana leaves to catch raindrops. Or use the collected water to raise a colony of minnows for food.

fig. 2

COMPASS

Tear out a page of the book and throw it into the air—there's a one-in-four chance the wind will carry it north. Therefore, throwing four pages into the air will give you a 100 percent chance!

fig. 3

KINDLING

◀ Set the book on fire (as you should anyway as soon as you're done reading it) to prevent others from gaining its advantages.

SUNDIAL

Construct a crude sundial by rolling the book up tightly and planting it in the ground to keep track of the most important survival knowledge of all—the approximate time of day. ▶

fig. 4

Writing a Best Seller

No one commands more fame and respect than a best-selling author. Combine one element from each of these categories to effortlessly bang out a hit book that initiates you into the champagne-guzzling and supermodel-dating world of professional writers:

STEP 1. FIRE UP THE TYPEWRITER. All classic books from *The Great Gatsby* to *Hamlet* were written on this loud, clunky, obsolete, timeless device.

STEP 2. WRITE WHAT YOU KNOW—or better yet, write about something exciting.

STEP 3. STICK TO A SCHEDULE. Force yourself to write every single day, unless you're tired, out of ideas, or there might be something good on TV.

STEP 4. CAPTURE THE HUMAN EXPERIENCE by capturing a bunch of humans and writing about the experience.

STEP 5. BE YOUR OWN HARSHEST CRITIC—and declare your manuscript to be the greatest book ever written. Imagine what the *less* harsh critics will say!

THE ELEMENTS of LITERATURE

Effortlessly bang out a literary masterpiece by combining one element from each of these categories:

RELATABLE BUT COMPELLING MAIN CHARACTER

☐ Crafty, precocious rapscallion whose naïve eyes see race in a way adults' can't

☐ Harvard professor who uses smarts to discover lost treasure buried under the ceiling of the Sistine Chapel

☐ Robot who doesn't know he's a robot

☐ Woman of some sort

FAMILIAR BUT EXCITING SETTING

☐ Smog and pickpocket-infested London where even homeless children wear top hats

☐ Suburban community where rich people complain about having it all

☐ Bronze Age space station

☐ World War I trench shared with sympathetic, introspective enemy solider who grows up to be Hitler

LASTING LITERARY SUCCESS

Every great author's goal is to write a novel so beloved that the profits from the movie version ensure they never have to write anything ever again.

EVIL BUT REDEEMABLE ANTAGONIST

☐ Endangered albino whale who isn't even doing anything bad on purpose

☐ Phonies

☐ Immoral businessman who puts science before God and a wall of laser-equipped gorillas before science

☐ Your diabolical twin cousin

SUBTLE BUT OVERT THEME

☐ Good vs. evil until good and evil have to team up to defeat a hockey team full of snobs

☐ The triumph of hope over poison

☐ "Always bet on black."

☐ Messages in bottles may not always find the person they were intended for, but will always find the person they were meant for

SATISFYING BUT BITTERSWEET CLIMAX

☐ The world is safe but at the cost of Integrity—Integrity being the name of the hero's classic Ferrari

☐ Wait a minute . . . the tollbooth was a phantom the entire time?!

☐ Fabio shows up

☐ Author breaks the fourth wall to solicit the reader's ideas for cool sequels.

READY-MADE SIMILES TO PAD YOUR PROSE

The most successful books use evocative language to trick their readers into having feelings. You can beef up an already-great manuscript using imagery from this master list of all known similes:

SLIPPERY as an eel

HARD as a rock

WISE as an especially smart owl

BLIND as any number of famous blues musicians

TALL as Rick Bigman, the world's biggest man

SCARY as the part in *Chucky* where you first see Chucky

HUNGRY as a guy who's only had a bagel today

COLORFUL as a peacock with a lot of life experience

ACCEPTABLE as a grown man who sleeps on a mattress on the floor

ALLURINGLY UNSANITARY as a kissing booth

DISAPPOINTED as most fathers

SICK as a dog

EXORBITANT as the veterinarian's proposed dog-surgery fee

MELANCHOLY as your final car ride with a sick dog

MIXING METAPHORS

For ultimate literary effectiveness, combine more than one metaphor for a savory stew that always hits a home run.

PERSUASIVE as Hollow Earth theories. What *is* in there?

NAUSEATING as a stick bug that you thought was just a stick

DARING as being shot out of a cannon

DARING as being shot *into* a cannon

SWEATY as a gas station pizza

SYMBOLIC as a rainbow being swallowed by a hurricane

LONELY as a teddy bear decomposing in the forest

COMMON as waking up during surgery

USEFUL as a list of similes

Your Last Words

Everything you say during your lifetime is just practice for the most dramatic moment of your life: your death. Use your last words as an opportunity to secure your financial future, leave behind an eternal mystery, or snag last-minute salvation, by following the three M's:

MONETIZED Your last words will have an attentive audience, receptive to your wisdom—a demographic coveted by advertisers. Sell your last words to the highest bidder and sail into the afterlife on a deathbed stuffed with money. E.g., "Life is but a bubble of time gradually floating to the top of a tall, cool glass of Pepsi. Drink Pepsi!"

MYSTERIOUS Leave an enigma for the ages by hinting at the location of a buried treasure that keeps your memory alive forever. E.g., "Not everyone would think to bury the *real Mona Lisa* at the top of one of the world's smallest mountains."

re**M**ORSEFUL You can atone for a life of misdeeds and self-ishness simply by apologizing at the last minute. E.g., "I subscribe to the tenets of whichever god is closest to this hospital."

FAMOUS LAST WORDS

By analyzing the final words of historical figures,
you can learn lessons on how to perfect your own parting remarks:

"EITHER THESE DRAPES GO OR I DO."
—Oscar Wilde

LESSON: Complain so much about petty annoyances
that everyone will be happy when you die.

"I AM NOT THE LEAST AFRAID TO DIE."
—Charles Darwin

LESSON: Lie.

"I'VE NEVER FELT BETTER."
—Douglas Fairbanks, Sr.

LESSON: While you should prepare a final pronouncement
that will echo throughout the ages, it's much more likely that
in your last moments you will have no clue what's going on.

GATHER YOUR LOVED ONES

There will never be a better place than on your deathbed to tell
your children which of them is your favorite.

Zoo Keeping

Once you've achieved success over your fellow man, you have an evolutionary obligation to extend your mastery over all the creatures of the Earth. Become Lord of All Beasts by keeping care—and control—of the animals you'll want for your private menagerie:

BEARS hibernate through the winter, but you can prevent them from entering this boring period of inactivity by pumping the summery tunes of Jimmy Buffett into their enclosure all year round at extremely high volume.

ELEPHANTS display their flashy, expensive ivory to make you feel poor; so stuff your own cheeks with money to show off your equivalent fortune.

GIRAFFES can't be housed adjacent to your bathroom—they'll use their long necks to peep at you while you're doing your business.

KILLER WHALES will only eat food they hunt and kill themselves so make sure to drop a **JAGUAR** in their tank every couple of weeks.

G.O.R.I.L.L.A.S. short for Gyroscopic Optical Rudimentarily Intelligent Life-Like Animatrons, replaced gorillas when they went extinct in 2002.

ZEBRAS cannot be tamed. Luckily, all they want to do is stand in one place and frequently fall asleep.

MAN, too, lives in a cage—the cage of his own longing. Be sure to get everything you want, all the time, to break out of this extremely real metaphorical prison.

How to Win at Everything Else

ARM WRESTLING

Plant your elbow on the table, your feet firmly on the ground, and your free hand engaged in a second arm-wrestling match to signal how ungodly confident you are.

ART APPRECIATION

Always look closely—for example, in Claude Monet's "Water Lilies," what appear to be beautifully rendered flowers are revealed up close to be nothing more than a mass of swirling protons, neutrons, and electrons.

BACCARAT

Just have a seat. This "game" is actually just a table where rich people sit, knowing they won't be bothered by poor people.

BECOMING A DOCTOR

Swear this take-at-home version of the Hippocratic Oath: "I swear first to do no harm. I swear second to do no harm . . . again–that's how important it is. When performing procedures learned from TV medical dramas, I swear to only do procedures from shows I watched all way to the credits, to make sure the doctors resolved their personal crises that were thematically parallel to the patient's condition. If any patient should die despite my best efforts, I swear to root around in their guts until I figure out what I did wrong. Finally, I swear to correct anyone who calls me Mister or Miss instead of Doctor."

CHARADES

Prepare a system with your partner in advance. For instance, shaking your left foot indicates the film *Footloose,* while shaking your right foot indicates that the answer is one of the other innumerable books, songs, or movies that could conceivably be chosen.

COMPOSING A SYMPHONY

Don't over-think it. Making music is so easy that even deaf people like Beethoven can do it.

CULTURAL PATRONAGE

Get your name on a symphony hall by finally killing that phantom of the opera.

DECISION MAKING

Never trust a knee-jerk reaction, unless your gut tells you otherwise.

DRESSING FORMALLY

You don't need money to look rich—just a good shovel and a map to the rich person's cemetery.

EVERY KNOWN SPORT

Remember, the team that has the most fun is the real winner, assuming that you derive fun solely from scoring more points than the other team.

EXCHANGING CURRENCY

Trade American dollars, British pounds, and Chinese yuan for the most powerful universal currency—your fists.

EXORCISING A GHOST

Sprinkle specter-repelling salt on the floor (ghosts hate salt because statistically most of them died of heart disease).

FISHING

Throw a toaster into a lake.

GETTING OUT OF A SPEEDING TICKET

When the officer asks you how fast you were going, reply "Exactly the speed limit. Plus several bonus miles per hour for good luck."

GIVING WEDDING ANNIVERSARY GIFTS

Remember, the tenth anniversary is tin, the twenty-fifth anniversary is two ferrets trained to form the shape of a heart, and the fiftieth anniversary gift is a real-life *Flintstones* car.

HEROISM

When you see a famous person or elected official, leap in front of them screaming "Nooo!" just in case they're about to get shot.

HIDING YOUR SPARE KEY

Hide your emergency key under a potted plant, a welcome mat reading "Not Concealing a Key," or a store-bought fake rock that you can use to smash any window and then climb in and unlock the door.

HORSEBACK RIDING

Steadily mount the horse by grabbing on to the strongest part of its anatomy, its eyelashes.

IDENTIFYING FALSE MESSIAHS

Be wary if your new god claims to be Jesus, but can only turn water into iced tea—and even then, needs to use Lipton powder.

KISSING

After you try French kissing (kissing with tongue), move on to American kissing (kissing with a mouthful of BBQ sauce).

LAST-MINUTE ENTERTAINING

Does a pack of hot dog buns covered in frosting count as a cake? Yes.

MUSIC APPRECIATION

In country music, the *country* they're talking about is America.

QUITTING A JOB

Give your employer two weeks' notice—two weeks to notice you're gone, that is.

SLOT-CAR RACING

Make the car go fast—but not *too* fast.

SPEAKING WITH A FOREIGNER

To win a conversation even in a language that you don't speak, simply talk louder than your opponent.

SPEED SKATING

Judges will knock five seconds off your time for every beer you chug per lap.

SPELLING BEE

It's always *E* before *I* except inside *pie*.

TALKING YOUR WAY PAST A BOUNCER

If you're not on the list, say "Did somebody order a Sex Magician?"

THE TWO HUNDRED-METER BREASTSTROKE

As soon as the starting pistol is fired, immediately sink to the bottom of the pool and simply run across.

WASHING AN INFANT

When you're done, throw out the baby, but keep that valuable bathwater!

YOUR DATE OF DEATH

In a rare moment of poetic natural symmetry, you will die at midnight on your 100TH birthday.

ACKNOWLEDGMENTS

The Braunstein-Weiner family, the Kibblesmith family, Steve Mockus, Scott Mendel, Julie Klausner, Anne Marie Sticksel, Andrew Peyton, Conner O'Malley, Chris Witaske, Mark Vannier, Mort Burke, George McAuliffe, Wes Haney, Jon Barinholtz, Jeff Altman, Brandon Hauer, Joe Kwaczala, Joe McAdam, Andrew Smreker, C.J. Toledano, AJ Conover, Christina Boucher, Kevin Lee, Chris Stephens, Ethan Peldo, Nathan Simmons, Dan Ronan, Megan Green, Aziz Oz Lalani, John Eisenrich, Nick Johnson, Mark Geary, Adam Rubin, Aidy Bryant, Timmy Skillings, John McGalagly, Todd Reichlmayr, Bobby Ellis, Chris Michalak, Mike Zell, Mick Napier, Jennifer Estlin, Mike Canale, Kyle Dolan, Tony Mendoza, Josh Walker, Sean Cusick, Rich Sohn, Rebecca Sohn, Cullen Crawford, Ben Kobold, Kristina Francisco, Jamison Webb, Julie Mossler, Andrew Mason, Aaron With, Dale Chapman, Craig Gore, Abraham Riesman, K. Thor Jensen, Ben O'Brien, Drew Swinburne, Erin Gleeson, Wham City, Ken Barnard, Blewt! Productions, Tyler Coates, John Holdun, Gabriel Roginic, Ruth Barabe, Jason Fabeck, Stephanie Kuhr, Nigel Shields, Hayley Rice, Cyrus, Alana Johnston, Rachel Olsen, Bryan DeGuire, Brooke Pobjoy, Naomi Odenkirk, Andy Downing, Jeff Dean, David Sidorov, JJ Shebesta, Liz Koe, Brett Blake, Andy Miara, Emily Candini, Genevieve Knapp, Mike Birnbaum, and Joe Meno.

If you see these people on the street, you're legally obligated to give them your copy of the book.

ABOUT THE AUTHORS

DANIEL KIBBLESMITH (@Kibblesmith) is a writer, cartoonist, and comedian in Chicago. He has written for *The Onion News Network*, *Blackbook*, and *Splitsider*, and contributed video to *Funny or Die* and *The Best Show* on WFMU, as well as appearing on Bravo's *The Millionaire Matchmaker*. His website is **Kibblesmith.com.**

....

SAM WEINER (@sam_weiner) is a Staff Writer for *The Onion News Network*. His work has appeared in *McSweeney's*, *Splitsider*, on NPR's *Marketplace*, and on stage at the Annoyance Theatre. He has also written and performed the one-man shows *Freddie Mercury: I'm Gay, I Have AIDS, and I'm Dead*, and *Pepsi Presents Sam Weiner*. He lives in Chicago.

....

For more content, updates, and exclusive, additional tips for winning, follow **@HowToWinBook** on Twitter.